*Liam O'Flaherty titles published by Wolfhound Press:*

*The Pedlar's Revenge and Other Stories* (1976)
*Skerrett* (1977) a novel
*All Things Come of Age: A Rabbit Story* (1977) (for children)
*The Test of Courage* (1977) (for children)
*The Ecstasy of Angus* (1978) a novella
*The Wilderness* (1978) a novel
*Famine* (1979) a novel
*The Black Soul* (1981) a novel
*Short Stories by Liam O'Flaherty* (1981) (paperback edition of *The Pedlar's Revenge*)
*Shame the Devil* (1981) autobiography

Limited first editions, handbound, signed and numbered
*The Pedlar's Revenge and Other Stories* (1976)
*The Wilderness* (1978)

**SHAME THE DEVIL**

# LIAM O'FLAHERTY

# SHAME THE DEVIL

WOLFHOUND PRESS

Published by Wolfhound Press,
68 Mountjoy Square, Dublin 1.

© 1981 Liam O'Flaherty
First edition: London, 1934
*All rights reserved. No part of this book may be reproduced or utilised in any form or by any means, electronic or mechanical, including photocopying, recording or by any information storage and retrieval system without prior permission in writing from the publisher.*

**British Library Cataloguing in Publication Data**

O'Flaherty, Liam
   Shame the devil.
   1. O'Flaherty Liam — Biography
   2. Authors, Irish — 20th century — Biography
   I. Title
   823'.912   PR6029.F5

ISBN 0-905473-64-7

Printed and bound in Great Britain
by Billing and Sons Limited
**Guildford**, London, Oxford, Worcester

I OFFER THIS DAGGER
TO MY ENEMIES

*At the moment of going to press, certain passages on pages 136 and 189 had to be deleted.*

I

MAN is a born liar. Otherwise he would not have invented the proverb: "Tell the truth and shame the devil." Pilate expressed in a single sentence the failure of the Roman Empire to frame a permanent civilization, within whose compass mankind could live happily, when he asked: "What is truth?" All intelligent men are now convinced that the attempt of Christianity to answer that question has been a failure. No one knows what is truth. And therefore, if I lie in attempting to tell the truth in this book, let the blame lie at the door of original sin rather than at the door of my conscience. If not the truth, it will be at least the log of my folly, and as such, perhaps, useful to those of my species who are equally cursed with original sin.

By the beginning of last summer, I was practically convinced that I had reached the end of my tether. To the casual observer, I would seem to be a lucky fellow. In the course of thirty-seven years I had made rather an astonishing journey from the naked rocks of the Aran Islands, where I was born in extreme poverty, to a position of some note in the literary world. I had visited, in one capacity or another, a large portion of the earth's surface. I had known war, hunger, sickness and disillusionment, without being seriously injured by any of them in my lust for life. I had married and reproduced my kind. Without ever having been rich, I had tasted all the most rich of the earth's fruits. I had loved where I willed, in the body and the spirit. I had felt exalted in the bed of a Circassian beauty and among the Norwegian snows, when the icicles were melting from the branches of the sunlit pines. I had no chains that the world could see, but roamed the continents at will.

And yet the devil had defeated me. I was convinced that I had pulled his tail too often. Having done all that benefited me nothing, except to convince me that there was no answer to Pilate's question. Like a vulture I had passed over the earth, devouring what came my way; only to find myself stranded in London, a gorged brute, who was to all appearances sombrely drinking himself to death in sordid taverns. I could not write. I was in debt. I depended on a few friends, whose attempts at helping me only helped to intensify my despairing cynicism. A frightful shame overwhelmed me whenever I found myself alone. I saw the gifts I had inherited from nature put to base uses, fouled by vicious habits and made impotent by alcohol, in which I sought forgetfulness. And then I fell ill.

It was not very serious, but it brought me to my senses. When a man is born on naked rocks like the Aran Islands, where the struggle for life against savage nature is very intense, the instinct for self-preservation is strong in him. His character tends towards morbidness and reckless adventure while he is in strong health, but the first sign of sickness makes him cling like a threatened limpet with a fast hold to the rock of life. Therefore, while I lay on my bed with a temperature of one hundred and three, this instinct for self-preservation came to my rescue.

"Drop everything and fly," it said. "If you stay here you are lost. Get back to your rocks where the devil can't tempt you. Banish from your mind everything that worries you. Get rid of all responsibilities. Make a fig at whatever duty you owe society and your dependants. Only one thing is important to a living being, and that is life. Preserve it."

At once I cast about for a means of escape. For many reasons, a return to the Aran Islands was out of the question. I would have to find a rock elsewhere. Rupert Grayson offered to arrange a trip to the West Indies on a cargo boat, but this proved to be out of the question as it meant waiting at least ten days. In any case, what I wanted was not to make a trip to the West Indies but to escape; particularly to escape the life of a writer. Then another friend offered to pay my passage to Mexico, but the Mexican authorities insisted that any individual intending to stay in their country must be a person of means. On inquiry at the travel agency, we found that practically every country in the world, even the most obscure ones, like Colombia and Venezuela, made similar demands. Five-sixths of the earth was closed to any unfortunate man in search of the opportunity of earning his bread by the sweat of his brow. It was a horrid revelation and it completed the process of bringing me to my senses.

Fifteen years previously I had fled from myself in a similar manner, but at that time the world was different. It was still possible for a penniless man to arrive in Winnipeg, Shanghai, Valparaiso or Sydney and find bread by labour. Now, however, capitalist finance has completed its enslavement of mankind, turning five-sixths of the earth into an internment camp, where poor slaves starve in the midst of untold wealth. It is no longer possible for a hungry slave to stow himself away on a ship bound for the Argentine and eat a cow from among the countless herds that roam the pampas. If he escapes imprisonment and reaches the cows, he will find that he cannot eat the leanest steak from one of them. They are all in pawn to some damned financier in Wall Street, or the City of London; to fellows who would rather slaughter them and leave their bodies to the vultures than allow a hungry man to fill his belly with their flesh.

There is no longer any haven of refuge on five-sixths of this mad earth, for any poor creature who wishes to escape from the horrors of capitalist civilization. He must stand his ground and fight it or go under. If he is barred by the collapse of capitalist finance from being a wage slave, he must become a brigand, or sell his talents in some whorish way, or die of hunger where he stands. Men of my profession generally take the choice of whoredom. While literature is still regarded as a noble art, those who pursue it are in the main a spineless horde, grovelling before some rump-fed boor, who has made millions by selling trashy newspapers, or else they are mouthpieces of the fantastic creeds that the mediocre mob has invented in its war against the human intellect. I have never been able to stomach any of these creeds, to the degree of becoming abject before it and writing to its bidding. On the other hand, I would rather rely on my vomit for sustenance than attempt to cater for the rump-fed boors.

"Then I must run to earth," I cried, "like a hard pressed fox, until I have re-organized my strength, weave cunning plots, throw by the board those vices that have placed me at the mercy of my enemies, to appear once more with shining eyes, a weasel to hypnotize the rabbits, who shall be forced to give me bread for my dreams."

I had at least established the identity of the devil. That was half the battle. The other half lay in getting rid of the habits that placed me at the devil's mercy. You must understand that the devil for a writer is a hankering after success and the fruits of success: luxury, social respectability and fame.

I said to my friend:

"Let me have the money for my fare to Mexico. With that I can live in France for a few months. During that time I'll either put myself right with my own conscience or realize that it's hopeless."

"Why choose France?" she said.

"Because it is the only country in Western Europe at the present time where a degree of civilization is prevalent among the mass of the population. It is the only country where there is a profound respect for the human intellect in itself. Therefore, I choose it as a sanatorium for my sick mind. If it cannot cure me, there is nothing left but to commit suicide or turn humanitarian."

"I hope it will help you," she said.

Indeed, as she saw me off at Victoria, I felt that she was in a worse position than myself. Worse? God's blood! What is my hell but a feeding ground for my defiant soul?

I felt so hurt by her pale, unhappy face as the train began to move. Then she smiled.

"Never mind, Liam. Things are bound to look up shortly, as Francis would say," she whispered.

I lost sight of her in the crowd on the platform and then I was alone, among trippers bound for their summer holidays on the Continent. I still felt weak as the result of my slight attack of influenza. My throat was very sore. A rash had broken out at the corners of my mouth. I was a melancholy sight. In my wallet I had a ticket for Paris, thirty-nine English pounds and fifty French francs. On the rack over my head was my suitcase and my typewriter. That constituted the total of my worldly wealth.

"Not a great deal," one might say, "as the result of thirty-seven years of life."

Particularly as I had borrowed the money. And the typewriter.

II

I HAD intended taking the night train from the Gare Montparnasse to Quimper in Brittany, but when I arrived in Paris I felt so ill that I decided to take the morning train instead. I took a taxi to a small hotel on the Boulevard Raspail. I walked into the hotel after asking the maid to fetch my luggage, which she did. At the best of times I am a careless and incompetent traveller, and I was particularly careless that evening owing to my illness; so I did not notice that my typewriter was missing until she brought the suitcase to my room.

"Where is my typewriter?" I asked her.

"What typewriter?" she said in astonishment.

"Good God!" I said. "Didn't you take my typewriter from the taxi?"

The poor woman was in great distress and she apologized profusely. She said that her husband was a taxi-driver, that he often found things left behind in his cab and that he invariably brought them to the police. She advised me to go in the morning to the police and inquire for my typewriter. It would certainly be there. I asked her to leave the room. Then I bolted the door and threw myself face downwards on the bed. The loss of the typewriter seemed to me to be the last straw. If I had not been ill, I would probably have gone out into the city and spent all my money in a foolish rage. Fortunately, being ill, I soon forgot the loss of the typewriter in the fear that my health was going to break down seriously. Nine years previously I had a nervous collapse which lasted for six months. Now I felt the same symptoms of its dreadful approach.

Suddenly, as I lay on the bed, my whole nervous system became strung to a very high pitch. I trembled from head to foot, there was a violent pain at the pit of my stomach and my brain watched intently. I remained perfectly still, holding my breath, waiting for some horror. At first I thought it was death, but presently I realized it was not death, but a remorse of conscience so strong that I was completely assimilated by it. The pain, the trembling and the fear of death vanished. I became unnaturally calm. All round me was silent and meaningless as in death. My imagination had transported me to a graveyard at the eastern end of my native island, so powerfully that I was present in it with all my senses.

A few years ago I went alone to this place in order to visit my mother's grave. At that time I was writing a novel called *The Puritan,* and on my way to the graveyard I became so absorbed in thinking about the novel that I did not realize where I was going or the purpose of my journey until I suddenly found myself standing over her grave. A little narrow mound of earth surmounted by a Celtic cross. On a black slab her name, my father's name, her age and a prayer for her soul were hewn. Sea-bleached grass grew sparsely on the little narrow mound. It seemed as if a knife were thrust into my bosom. The man standing by the grave felt exalted by the knife-thrust, for he was drunk with creative enthusiasm. I, however, felt its pain, for that fire was now dead in me. He smiled and looked about him, looting the scene with fierce, avaricious eyes, impervious to remorse, gloating over the majesty of the human intellect that can transcend the tragedy of death and turn it into ecstasy. But I stood there as a penitent outcast, begging to be received once more into the fold.

Hot with unshed tears I looked round the desolate burial-place, a crumbling sandhill within a sea of sand, and the sea itself beyond, white in the shimmering sunlight. The burial-place was covered with rank shore grass, except where the gravestones lay. Some of the stones were spotted with red and grey lichen. Briars grew in the shelter of the older stones. There was a ruined church, sunk to its gables in the sandy earth. Holy men had said Mass there over a thousand years ago, but now it was engulfed by death. Death had engulfed it in common with the monks who worshipped there and all the people who were buried in the yard during the ensuing centuries, turning them to sand, except for the spare grass and briars that grew from their rotting flesh and bones upon this arid soil. Even the earth itself was being devoured, sucked into the bowels of the gnawing sea. And my mother? What of this woman in whose womb I had taken substance and the breath of life? A few parched blades of rank grass growing on a little mound by the edge of the advancing sea.

In agony I recalled my first memory of her, telling me the story of her marriage while she combed my hair. She told it as one tells a fairy-tale to amuse a child, how her handsome young lover came by night on horseback to her father's house and abducted her, at the very moment when another suitor from the mainland was there asking for her hand; how she was married at dawn in the chapel and went to live in an old deserted house in our village, penniless and unforgiven by her parents. Her fairy-tale ended with her marriage. After that, her life was a tale of hardship and misery, an endless struggle to find food for her many children.

And yet how gay she was in spite of all her suffering! Even when there was no food in the house, she would gather us about her at the empty hearth and weave fantastic stories about giants and fairies, or mime the comic adventures of our neighbours, until our hungry little bellies were sick with laughter. No suffering could dull the divine enthusiasm with which life inspired her. She could weep over the beauty of a little flower growing from a speck of dirt on a naked rock as well as for her own sufferings. A lady-bird toiling up a blade of grass brought to her lips a prayer of thanksgiving. A majestic sea-plant, waving in a pool at low tide, excited her imagination to discourse for hours on the wonders of the sea, as she sat with me upon a sunny rock.

Then, when my imagination, fed on these fancies, began its own adventures at her knee, recounting what I saw on the crags, the cliffs and by the seashore, how I conversed with eagles, was invited to a mermaid's cave and all the wonders that I saw therein, or how I stole a lark's wings and saw Heaven from the summit of a golden cloud, tears of joy flowed from her eyes and she said God had blessed me with a holy mind. And then the angel of revolt entered into me. My tales became more fierce, until one day, when I was about nine, I terrified her. I rushed into the house from school and told her that I had seen a labourer called McDonagh murder his wife in a potato garden. I described most luridly how he attacked her because she had lost his tobacco, how he struck her with his spade on the head many times, blaspheming joyously at each stroke, how she sank into a furrow, where she bled so profusely that the ensuing blows made her gore splash into her murderous husband's face, how her body was so fat that the murderer had to dance on it in order to make it fit into the furrow, how he covered it carefully with earth and then thanked God, with his head bowed and his eyes to Heaven, for having rid him of the slut.

My description was so vivid and sustained by such a horrified expression that my mother rushed out to warn the neighbours of the event. But the first person she saw was McDonagh's wife, knitting peacefully on her doorstep. Then she came back, looked at me and burst into tears. She made me go on my knees with her, to ask that God, in His Divine mercy, should cure my mind of this morbid leprosy. I wept with her while we were on our knees, but I afterwards walked along the clifftops and shouted in the face of the strong wind that came up from the radiant sea. And from that day I hid my dreams. I became a dual personality. The one wept with my mother and felt ashamed of his secret mind. The other exulted in this mind and began to dream of greatness. And as my mind grew strong and defiant, I became timid and sensitive in my relationship with the people about me. I became prone to dreaming, quick at my schooling, ashamed of vulgar profanity and rowdy conduct. So that my relatives and all the neighbours understood that I had a vocation for the priesthood. Nor did I deny this although it made me feel ashamed, for I despised the priesthood and thought it was more noble to do the ordinary chores of our society as a lusty male, to till the earth, to be strong and brave at sea, to marry and beget children, to raise one's voice with authority in the councils of one's fellows.

Then a priest belonging to the Holy Ghost Order came to spend a holiday with our schoolmaster, of whom he was a relative by marriage. The schoolmaster drew his attention to my zeal for scholarship. The priest brought me for many walks about the island and finally suggested I should become a postulant for his Order. I understood little of what this implied, but I understood him well when he explained that in this way I should be able to get my education practically free. So I agreed, and my delighted relatives managed to collect the small sum of money required. And in my thirteenth year I was sent as a postulant to the scholasticate of the Holy Ghost Order at Rockwell in the county of Tipperary, to be trained as a priest for the conversion of African negroes to the Roman Catholic religion.

After four years at this scholasticate the time came for me to take the soutane. I refused to do so. I had no interest in interfering with the negroes of Africa and I did not want to suffer the humiliation of wearing a priest's womanly rig. The director of the scholasticate was furious and accused me of deception, saying I had pretended for four years to have a vocation in order to sneak my education cheaply. As he was probably right I said nothing. At the end of the term I went home. However, through the influence of my friend, the priest, I went in the following term to another college belonging to the Order at Blackrock in Dublin. This time I was no longer in the scholasticate but among the ordinary boarders. I stayed a year at this college and then entered the Dublin diocesan seminary at Clonliffe through my friend's influence. By then I had no longer any desire to be a priest, either secular or regular, but I agreed in order not to disappoint my mother. But again I found the wearing of the soutane too much for me. I detested the other students and the priests in charge, who were soon outraged by the violence of my opinions. After a few weeks, I danced on my soutane, kicked my silk hat to pieces, spat on my religious books, made a fig at the whole rigmarole of Christianity and left that crazy den of superstitious ignorance. For a short time I attended lectures at University College, Dublin, where I had won a scholarship. Then I joined the Irish Guards and went to the war.

This was a far greater blow to my relatives than my refusal to become a priest, and it was the event in my life most responsible for the outcast position in which I now find myself. May the devil be praised! No matter how we may curse the war, my generation was fortunate in being given this wonderful lesson in the defects of the European system of civilization. Had it not been for my participation in the war, I might still be a petty Irish nationalist, with a carped outlook on life, one of those snivelling patriots who would prefer an Irish dunghill to an English flower garden in full bloom. Be that as it may, when I came home from the war in 1918, I was regarded as a pariah and a fool and a renegade. Those who did not hate me for having worn an English uniform pitied me, which was equally unpleasant. I left the country once more and tramped around the world for three years. I returned a second time an ill man, without money, disillusioned. I stayed some months on the island and then plunged into the revolutionary movement, with mad inconsequence. In the early part of 1922 I seized the Rotunda in Dublin with a small army of unemployed men. We hoisted the red flag over the building and held it for some days. Then we were driven out and I fled to Cork with two companions.

This adventure, which caused a great sensation in the public press, completed my ostracism. Ever since then, I have remained, in the eyes of the vast majority of Irish men and women, a public menace to faith, morals and property, a Communist, an atheist, a scoundrel of the worst type, a man whom thousands would burn at the stake if they had the courage.

Now as I lay on my bed, I accused myself most bitterly for having allowed myself to be regarded in this light by my people. I accused myself of having broken my mother's heart; for indeed she died shortly after my adventure in the Rotunda. I thought how comforting it would be to recant my heresies, to bow the knee to the gods of my country and to be taken back into the fold as a lost sheep that had been found again. Thus I would gain peace, honour and prosperity. I would feel the joy of forgiveness, of being at one with my tribe. I would have the simple beliefs of my forefathers to shelter me against doubt and tribulation.

Then suddenly I was taken with a great rush of blood into my bosom, so that I panted with its heat. The horror of the vision disappeared and the graveyard was transformed into a joyous place of great beauty. A host of birds made music there. Luxuriant plants had sprung to life from out the barren sand. Great banks of sweet-smelling flowers shut out the desolate stones. The air was heavy with exquisite perfume. And in the midst of all this loveliness I saw my sister Agnes, who was buried near my mother, rise up before me. She was the playmate of my infancy. She had loved, married, borne children and died in the smiling April of her beauty. Even lecherous death had not stayed her laughter. He chose consumption for her slaughter, and its devouring heat maintained the blushes in her cheeks until her end. She laughed and sang on her deathbed. Death took her as a laughing bride, and now the beauty of her life and death gave me wings. I soared in spirit from the sombre yard of death and boarded a great ship, whose white sails tipped the clouds. In her I coursed upon the ocean, making great way, until she suddenly vanished into space and I sat up on my bed with a violent start.

Recant? Crave forgiveness? Clip the wings of my fancies, in order to win the favour of the mob? To have property and be esteemed? To attend banquets as a guest of honour? To kiss the Pope's toe and win a title? Ho! Devil! Rather the whore of London, shining in her jewels, than such an unwashed nun, canting her sombre superstitions. Better to be devoured by the darkness than to be hauled by dolts into an inferior light.

## III

In the morning I awoke exhausted by this dream. I felt terribly depressed. Again I felt urged to leave everything and wander away. But where? On consideration it became obvious to me that the only direction in which I could wander was to the police station in search of my typewriter.

"I'll get my typewriter," I said, "and leave at once for Brittany."

I thought it would be an easy matter getting my typewriter. Last winter I left an overcoat in a London taxi on my way home late at night. The following morning, on applying to the police, I was immediately presented with the coat. In Paris I had quite a different experience. In an ante-room I was pounced upon by a clerk, whose eagle eye recognized me as a foreigner. He beckoned me to his desk, and having made certain of my nationality, he offered to simplify my difficulties.

"What difficulties?" I said rather angrily, clearly understanding what the fellow had in mind.

He shrugged his shoulders and said in a melancholy but rather threatening tone:

"Oh! Very well. If you look at it that way . . ."

"I would," I said, "if I were not in a desperate hurry to get out of Paris. Is twenty enough?"

He did not say anything, but he seemed quite pleased when I dropped two ten-franc pieces on the table by his elbow. In fact, he went to the trouble of pushing a piece of blotting-paper over them with a pencil. Then he filled a long form for me, after getting the particulars of my loss.

"Call in here to-morrow morning," he said, "and you will very likely get your typewriter."

"To-morrow?" I cried in disgust. "Can't I get it now?"

"Impossible," he said. "To-morrow, perhaps, or the day after. One never knows. Paris is a large city. Good day, sir."

At that moment he had caught sight of an American, to whom he beckoned feverishly. I looked at the American and felt like warning him to keep his money in his pocket until he got whatever he was searching for, but I thought better of it. So I rushed out of the place, cursing the French Government for paying its officials so poorly that they must rely on their tips for enough money to buy themselves drink and bed-money for their mistresses. However, the anger aroused in me by this incident did me a great deal of good, for it dispelled my torpor of the morning, and I went along the streets, swearing in a most hearty fashion.

In this mood I found myself standing in front of Notre-Dame Cathedral, at a moment when a gang of priests were entering by the main door. A workman who was idling there thought I was cursing the priests and he hailed me as a comrade.

"They are black vermin," he said. "They are social parasites."

"Who?" I said gruffly, being rather irritated by his manner.

"Those black crows," he cried. "See how fat they are, the pigs, while men like me, that fought in the trenches, we are starving, we are skin and bones. Last night I was struck on the head by a gendarme while I was demonstrating for my class. It's not enough to get rid of the priests. They are but one manifestation of bourgeois tyranny. They must all go, comrade. Could I have a cigarette?"

He was a ragged fellow, with the blotched face of a drunkard. He had a mean and furtive expression. His railing voice was offensive to the ear. I gave him one franc and said:

"Hast thou not heard that God is dead?"

He looked at me in astonishment.

"Yes," I cried. "He is dead. Go and tell your comrades. Run through the streets shouting the news. Rejoice. Make merry."

The man shrank from me and then quickly turned on his heel, muttering to himself. I watched him move away and then I began to laugh. He looked back and shook his head at me angrily, for he thought I was making fun of him, but I was really laughing at myself. His denunciation of the Church had shown me how righteous anger can degenerate into a mean hatred. I saw in this ragged, drunken, mendicant proletarian of the twentieth century, puffed with cant phrases about "the good world to come," an exact reproduction of the Roman proletarian who riled at the rich Imperial priests and mumbled Christian rites in the catacombs and dreamt of "the good world to come." *Le Bon Dieu est Mort. Vive le Bon Dieu.* But the good world never comes for the proletarians, who hail the death of God as a prelude to an atheism, under which the last shall be first. A new God is always in existence before the death of the old God. That is why I told the man to rejoice and to go through the streets shouting his joy. For if the old God is dead, then all good men should urge their brothers to worship the new God, lest an interregnum of atheism should bring disaster on the world; as on a hive in which there is no queen.

I myself have erred in this respect. When I became a Communist after the war, I did so for practically the same reasons that this ragged drunkard, skulking outside the beautiful cathedral of Notre-Dame, was riling at the injustice of modern society. As if a society could exist without injustice! As if, indeed, justice could exist without its opposite! No more than night could exist without day. I could only remember the lice of the war and its hunger and its mangling of beautiful youth, in body and soul. Although I had escaped the war, I had been numbed by its shells. I could only see it as a giant manifestation of society's corruption rather than the birth of a new civilization bursting from the womb of an old and decadent one. The monstrous guns that belched their loads of iron and of poisonous gas showed that the God of this new civilization could shout louder than Jove or than Jehovah. But I was afraid of their power and I wanted them destroyed. So I cried with all the other terrified and weary ones: "Let there be no more war. Man is a wicked animal. He must not be allowed to toy with dangerous weapons." Like an early Christian, my Communism became an adulation of rags and suffering, a suspicion of grandeur and refinement. I wanted to pull down the mighty from their thrones instead of raising the lowly to the same degree of culture and wealth as the mighty.

Indeed, I soon found that I was unfitted to be the adherent of any political creed and that I could not believe in any God. According as the creative impulse grew stronger in me, I found my Communist associates as bigoted, narrow-minded and insufferable as Roman Catholic fanatics or reactionary Conservatives. Finally I went to Russia and became convinced that I reacted as violently towards fervent Communists as towards members of the Primrose League. As far as I am concerned, they are all satellites of throned humbug. The only difference in my attitude towards them is that I know the Communists are bringing into being a more efficient organization of society. They are liberating man from enslavement by the machine and making him the master of it. They are liberating man from the threat of famine, and by so doing they are going to enlarge his intellectual powers to an enormous extent. When they have done so the world will be a better place, but by then I shall be dead. I shall have sung my song and gone my way.

So I thought as I strolled from Notre-Dame to Montparnasse. And I felt gay. I felt that I had already gone a long way from London and from my despair. For the moment at least the bitterness of defeat had gone out of my soul, and I did not even feel cross with the clerk who had inveigled twenty francs from me. In fact, I rather admired his cleverness.

In this excellent mood I sat down on the terrace of the Café du Dome at Montparnasse and ordered a cup of coffee. It was noon and the place was crowded. As a rule one hears nearly every civilized language spoken at this café, but this time my ears soon became aware that German was easily predominant. I became interested and looked about me, examining the faces. I have rarely in my life seen such a sordid spectacle. The vast majority of them were Jews, of a type that is rarely seen in Western Europe. They were almost negroid, but without the solemn dignity of the negro countenance. They were shabby, and one noticed their shabbiness unpleasantly because they were of such mean physique. The violence of their gestures and the crudeness of their babbled speech was in some manner repulsive. They kept jumping about, shouting at one another and causing such a vulgar uproar that instead of feeling pity for the poverty of their condition, one felt a brutal desire to knock their heads together or stamp on them.

While I was watching them, a girl whom I knew came and sat at my table. I asked her who these people were.

"Ach!" she said, with a grimace of disgust. "They are filthy German Jews that have been kicked out by the Hitlerites. I hate them. I hate the Germans, too, but they are quite right in persecuting the Jews. The Jews should all be exterminated."

This point of view surprised me and made me feel irritated with the woman.

"But you are a Jewess yourself," I said. "Why should you want your own race exterminated?"

"I'm not a Jewess," she said angrily. "My mother was a Rumanian of pure Rumanian stock. My father was a Jew, but that does not matter. Very likely I am a bastard. I hope so, because I don't want to have any Jewish blood in me. They are a low race. Parasites. They are like flies buzzing on a dunghill. Wherever there is corruption they are to be found. Ach!"

She shrugged her shoulders.

"I do not greatly admire the Jews as a race," I said, "but I do certainly think that they deserve a better place in the sun than the Germans, whose contribution to human civilization seems to me of very doubtful value. I think that a Germany governed by Jews might be a lesser danger to human happiness than a Germany governed by Prussians. Why not exterminate the Prussians and plant their country with Jews? It would at least be an interesting experiment. The Prussians have given nothing to Europe except the goose-step, brutality and bad manners, whereas the Jews . . ."

"What have the Jews given Europe?" she cried angrily.

"Karl Marx," I said.

"Marx," she cried, "was a fool. Just a typical, low Jew."

"Don't talk nonsense," I said. "One-sixth of the globe is already governed on the basis of his teachings, and on the remainder of the globe his influence is enormous. To denounce him as a fool merely brands you as a thoughtless and ignorant woman. You have never read a word of Marx."

"Have you?"

"Yes, I have; and what's more I have tried to beat his beer drinking record without success. He and Friedrich Engels drank their way from the bottom of Tottenham Court Road to The Spaniards on Hampstead Heath, and then he beat Engels at a game of chess. If that does not prove him to be a great man, there is no such thing as a test of greatness."

"And that's all you know about him," she cried viciously, "that he was a drunkard like yourself? Why are you now drinking coffee instead of beer? Have you got venereal disease?"

"I refuse to get angry," I said, "and I insist on telling you about Marx. I first heard of him from a Jesuit priest called Finlay, who was professor of political economy at University College, Dublin. He was lecturing on value, and when he came to the Marxian definition, he said that Marxism was, of course, ridiculous nonsense. I stood up and asked him to explain why it was ridiculous nonsense. He was nettled by my question and refused to give any sort of answer, except to repeat that Marxism was ridiculous nonsense. After the lecture I went to the National Library and took out *Das Capital*. I became at once enthralled by it. I attended no more lectures, but I spent ten hours in the library each day for a fortnight studying Marx. At the end of the fortnight I understood the first few chapters. As a result I understood the construction of modern society and the correct manner of approaching the study of human history. In other words, I understood life."

My friend laughed loudly and said:

"What a liar you are! As if a creative writer could be interested in political economy, or have to learn about life from a German Jew!"

"On the contrary," I said, "it is more necessary for

a creative writer to know political economy than for a painter to have eyesight. The writer who remains indifferent to the social movements of his time, or fails to understand them, could never write anything of value. A writer of the present day must be a Marxian, a worshipper of the machine, for Marxism and the machine are the power and the explanation of our era."

"That's all nonsense," she said. "Mussolini and Hitler are going to put an end to the Marxian illusion."

"Indeed!" I cried, getting heated. "I respect Mussolini, as a magnificent sort of modern Condottiere; Sigismondo Malatesta, Muzio Attendolo and Al Capone thrown into one. Italy produces Cæsars in the same prodigal way that the Jews produce Messiahs. And I must say that this modern Cæsar, although not in the same class as Julius or Napoleon Bonaparte, seems to have done a great deal towards raising the dignity of his country. He has made Italy one of the great European powers. But is that a proof that Marxism is an illusion? On the contrary, Mussolini owes his rise to power to Marxism. He was educated on Marxism and his Fascist State is a Marxist abortion. The financiers chose this Marxian renegade as their protector against the Communist spectre which haunted Italy in 1920. They made him their Condottiere. In the same way, German financiers and feudal barons have chosen the housepainter, Adolf Hitler, as their Condottiere. Even Hitler, although the man has no pretensions to education, except in the misty caverns of his own mind, also toys with the Socialist teachings of Marx. He is, forsooth, a National Socialist. But neither he nor his more talented

Italian comrade are anything more than outstanding heretics against the true faith. They will be swept aside like skittles before the advance of the Marxist machine, descending on Europe from its Russian stronghold."

"Bah!" she cried. "The Russians are an inferior race."

I finally lost my temper with her, and in order to prevent myself saying something personally offensive, I changed the subject and spoke of my typewriter.

"Ho!" she cried. "You'll never get it. The French are all thieves. They are a low race."

That was too much for me.

"The cheek of you!" I cried. "You all come here to France, a rabble from all over the world, to escape the horror of life in your own wretched countries, to enjoy French culture and the amenities of French life. You live here in peace and security, protected by the French army from the savage hordes that menace the French frontiers, like needy robbers hanging about the walls of a rich city. And yet, instead of being grateful, you sneer at France. You should all be guillotined."

I walked away from the place. The guillotine? Yes. The guillotine! But would I escape it myself? This woman who spent her life sitting on the terrace of a Parisian café, posing as an intellectual and sneering at life, seemed to me typical of the majority of European intellectuals.

"They sneer at the corruption of society," I cried, as I strode along towards the Luxembourg gardens, "but they are careful not to associate themselves actively with the purifiers, lest the Paper Barons who feed them might take offence. And because they are cowards, their work is lifeless, barren and trivial. And am I myself any better than these writers whom I consider to be scoundrels and hypocrites, the exquisite panders who are the literary idols of the educated European bourgeoisie to-day? I am neither exquisite nor a pander, and I am not the idol of any class. Yet I trimmed my sails to get bread. But what am I talking about?"

Suddenly the fear and trembling of the previous night again took hold of me. Beads of perspiration started out on my forehead. The soreness of my throat became intense. My nose began to bleed. When I raised my foot to advance in my walk I felt timid of planting it again on the pavement. I glanced furtively at the people who passed, feeling that I was under their hostile observation and that they might fall on me, imprison me and then put me to death. For what crime? Ha! Ha! Why had I been shouting like a fool on the terrace of the Dôme about Fascists and Communists? These warring factions meant nothing to me. They were all hostile. I was really indifferent to their objectives, which are meaningless to me as a poet, who is only concerned with catching the wraith of beauty and bringing her to a life of flesh and blood with words; beautiful singing words. Why had I said to the man that God was dead?

And then again I saw myself in flight, a lean man with terrified, furtive eyes, wearing a shabby trench-coat, with a revolver strapped between his shoulder-blades, arriving in Liverpool on a cargo-boat in June 1922. I tried feverishly to drive him away, but he kept coming back, and then I knew that I must face him, talk to him and find out what he wanted. He was myself and therefore I must gain the mastery over him, or he would remain there for ever at the back of my mind, to rush at me when I was in distress.

And as soon as I agreed to face him I grew calm. I had by then entered the gardens. I sat down on a bench beside a wide, sanded avenue lined with trees. A great number of children were playing tennis all along the avenue and their cries were gay. Soothed by their merry cries and their innocent beauty, I looked at the sand and whispered to the phantom:

"Now what have you to say?"

The scene was now more terrible than the graveyard at Killeany. It was O'Connell Street in Dublin, during the capture of the Republican headquarters by the Free State troops in June 1922. I was standing on the south side of the bridge with a comrade. We had been disbanded on the previous day and we were now watching the destruction of the hotels where headquarters were still holding out. The Free State soldiers were throwing incendiary bombs from across the street into the hotels. There was a rattle of machine-gun and rifle fire. A cordon had been drawn all round the doomed buildings, and crowds of people stood outside the barriers, watching the scene, as at a public entertainment. Then I heard an old woman in a group behind me say:

"Did ye hear that bloody murderer, Liam O'Flaherty, is killed, thanks be to God?"

"Who?" said another old woman.

"Liam O'Flaherty," said the first. "The man that locked the unemployed up in the Rotunda and shot them unless they spat on the holy crucifix. The man that tried to sell Dublin to the Bolsheviks."

"Is he dead?" said a man.

"Shot through the heart this morning in Capel Street," said the old woman. "The Lord be praised for ridding the country of that cut-throat. Ho, me hearties! Give the bastards what's comin' to them."

The old woman cheered the soldiers who were now running across the street to take the headquarters by storm. A mass of flames shot up from the roofs of the buildings through a thick bank of smoke. A great cheer came from the watching people. I nudged my comrade and we walked away together.

"I'm going," I said. "There's nothing more to be done."

"Where?" he said.

"To England."

"Surely to God ye're not quittin'," he said. "It's only startin' yet. We'll have flyin' columns in action within a couple o' days. Then the fun'll start."

"No," I said. "That old woman was right. I'm dead."

A few days later I arrived in Liverpool. There I stayed for a fortnight, trying to make up my mind what to do. Indeed, I felt dead. I was twenty-six. I felt it was time to adopt some profession in life. I had abandoned hope in the coming of the revolution. But what could I do? In this quandary I received a letter from a friend in London, inviting me to stay at her mother's house. Her mother kept a shop near Hyde Park. She was a remarkable woman, and although of

Conservative opinions at that time, she had befriended a number of Irish revolutionaries. I accepted the invitation and went to London. The daughter, who had read some articles I had written for revolutionary papers, advised me to take up writing as a profession. So she got me an old typewriter and I began to write short stories. I also wrote a novel. Both the novel and the short stories were crude nonsense, as I had no knowledge whatsoever of the art of writing fiction. Several times during the first few weeks, when the trashy stories kept being returned by the editors to whom they were submitted, I wished to give up the business, but my friend urged me to persevere. She had become attached to me and did not want me to go to America, as I wished to do.

By then I felt that I had got myself into a difficult position, but I could see no way of escape from it. I saw that the girl's attachment was serious and I did not want to give her pain; yet I could not force myself to tell her that I did not love her. In the meantime the affairs of the shop were getting into difficulties and the mother found my presence in the house a burden. Even yet I shudder when I think of the humiliation I suffered during those six months. I hardly ever saw anybody outside the family and their few friends. I wrote all day in the basement and then stood in the evenings among the arguing crowds at the Marble Arch, or else wandered about the Park, gloomily meditating on my position.

Then I began to write another novel. One morning a humorous paper had returned a manuscript with some sarcastic verses attached. Infuriated by these verses, I dashed out of the house and walked about the streets, determined never to write another word of this trash. In order to console myself for my unhappiness I began to think of my native island, where life was so peaceful and beautiful compared with the turmoil and artificiality of London. That day there was a heavy fog. The streets and even the pavements were heavy with mud, which was thrown up in showers by the heavy wheels of buses and lorries. It was so dark at noon that the lamps were lit. And I thought how beautiful it would be to stand on a cliff in Aran, watching the great waves come thundering to the shore, while the pure wind swelled my lungs. Then I was possessed by a tender joy and I felt one with the harmony of the simple life of my people. This joy found words. While I was walking down Praed Street I suddenly realized that if I must write, I must be the spokesman of that life; for I loved it, and one can only write inspired by love. So I rushed back to the house, sat down to the typewriter and began to write about Aran.

It seemed as if a dam had burst somewhere in my soul, for the words poured forth in a torrent. They came joyously and I felt exalted by their utterance, just as I used to feel when telling my mother some fantastic tale in my infancy. I was raised by them from the sordidness and unhappiness of my environment to the fairyland of creative passion. The girl and her mother were astonished at the change in me; for now my wild laughter came to them from the basement, as I paused for a few minutes in my typing to revel in some oddity. I remained drunk in that way for a fortnight. My exuberance shut out all thought of the world about me.

I lived entirely among my characters and was only vaguely conscious of those to whom I spoke in real life. I slept, drank, ate food and walked about merely to sustain my energies for the consumption of the magnificent feast of which I was partaking. And then the frenzy exhausted itself. One morning I awoke to find that I no longer believed in what I was writing. I did not want to continue it. The vision had vanished. I wanted to run away and hide myself. I sat down to breakfast morbid and silent, glaring at mother and daughter with fierce eyes, from which the light of ecstasy had departed.

This mood lasted for three days, and the mother, who had been as enthusiastic as her daughter about my book while my ecstasy made me such a pleasant and exciting companion, again began to find me a burden in the house. I could not write, and sat in silence in the basement most of the day. The daughter was in tears and tried to rouse me to activity. But her efforts were useless. I would have gone at that time if I had had the energy to move; but the ecstasy had exhausted me physically as well as mentally. And then it suddenly returned of its own accord. I began to write once more.

Now, however, it was an effort to write and I could not become unconscious of my surroundings. One part of me was among my characters, a subconscious part, while another part was very conscious of the mother and daughter and of my dependence on them. I no longer wrote for the love of writing, of pouring out words and gambolling among the fantastic creatures of my imagination. I wanted to finish a novel, to sell it for money and free myself from these two women. And this sordid motive robbed the work of all pleasure. I had begun to pay for the joy of being able to create, and I paid in anger and indignation. It was about this time that I had my first short story accepted by a newspaper called the *New Leader*. For a few days this success helped to cheer me, but afterwards my gloom became even more intense. At last my position in the house became impossible. I quarrelled with the old woman and went to live in a garret in Fitzroy Street. That was in February 1923. All the money I had was the three guineas which I had been paid by the *New Leader*.

The daughter had not lost faith in me. Indeed, her attachment was intensified by the precariousness of my position and she did everything in her power to help me. Even so, I lived in great straits, mostly on a diet of pease-pudding, potatoes and mutton at twopence per pound. I cooked the potatoes and the mutton as a stew in my room on a little gas-ring, with the result that the place became full of bugs, which tormented me during the night. The room was so small that I had to sit on the bed in order to be able to use the typewriter. Across the landing lived a street prostitute who was suffering from an advanced stage of pulmonary tuberculosis. The poor wretch's coughing was an agony to me and yet I could do nothing to help her. As she stayed out until the early hours of the morning trying to earn a few shillings, the noise of my typewriter would disturb her sleep in the morning; so I could not write until noon. That being the case, I spent the mornings tramping around Fleet Street looking for work. The weather was bad and my shoes leaked, so that I was soon coughing as badly as my friend the prostitute;

nor did my solicitation of the editors in Fleet Street profit me any more than her nocturnal prowling. As a result of a fortnight's touting, I only earned five shillings, paid me by the *Daily Herald* for a small news paragraph.

In the meantime I had finished and re-written my novel, and immediately brought it to a publisher's office. When I had done so I lost heart. I felt ill and exhausted. I was half starved and crazy for want of sleep, what with working late into the night and being tortured by the bugs. Finally, I was worried by the state of my friend's affection. One morning, about ten days after I had submitted my manuscript, I decided to leave my garret, go down to the east end and try to stow away on a ship for New York. On my way I called at the publisher's office to collect my manuscript. I did not want to leave behind me what had given me so much joy, hope, pain and misery. To my astonishment they told me in the office that the publisher himself wished to see me.

"I want my manuscript," I said gruffly, thinking they were making fun of me.

Or else they were about to hand me over to the Free State authorities. You must understand that the Civil War still lasted in Ireland, and that during all these months I had spent in London I had often gone out carrying a revolver in my pocket, feeling that I was being pursued by political enemies. Sometimes this mania of being pursued by assassins had been so intense that I sat up in bed for hours, my revolver in my hand, listening and watching. Indeed, my desire to fly the country and stow away on a ship to New York had been largely inspired by this fear. Three days previously, on getting up, I looked out through the window of my garret and saw on a newspaper poster across the street that there had been a great round-up of Irish Republicans in London. A policeman was standing near the poster, looking towards my house. I at once felt certain that he was waiting to catch me. I closed the window and sat on my bed for nearly two hours, afraid to leave the house. It was then I had decided on flight.

Now when I was invited to go upstairs to the publisher's private office, the same fear returned. Were there detectives up there waiting to pounce on me? Had I written something in my manuscript that would give a handle to my persecutors? What persecutors? The kind English faces of those in the office, who were smiling in gentle amusement at my distraught appearance, reassured me and I followed one of them upstairs. Then, indeed, my astonishment was intense, for the publisher received me as an important personage. I stood before him in my ragged trench-coat and leaking shoes, while he told me that he wished to publish my manuscript.

I sat down, hardly able to meet his eyes or answer his remarks; so strange did it seem to be treated in this manner. He read me a letter from Edward Garnett advising the acceptance of my manuscript, not because it was likely to sell, but because it was the work of a promising young writer. It is impossible to describe the exalted joy that this news gave me. The joy of a lover on realizing that his love is returned is nothing compared to it. I was completely beside my wits. I was convinced that I was already rich, famous, a man of genius. The ten pounds which the publisher gave me as an advance on royalties seemed an enormous fortune which it was impossible to spend. I wandered through the streets, a little astonished that people passed me without recognition of my exalted merit. And then, when I became a little more calm, I thought of the girl who had helped me to produce this novel, which had raised me at one stroke from unexampled misery to supreme joy.

I rushed to her house, told her the exciting news, went on my knee, kissed her hand and asked her to marry me. She wept with joy, and indeed her excitement was as great as my own. Like children we began to make plans for the future. Even her mother shared our enthusiasm. Impressed by the change in my circumstances, she gave her blessing to our union, and it was decided that we should get married as soon as possible. Then I returned to my garret to dream. What a night! The hapless woman next door, being more ill than usual, was unable to set forth on her miserable adventure, so I gave her some money and told her to make merry, for I was now a rich man. At first she wept in gratitude, and then her thin, flushed face became hard and I saw envy in her sick eyes. She felt that I had escaped the pit where we had been comrades in misery. But I was indifferent to her envy. I sat in my room until the early hours of the morning, unable to sleep, brooding over the magnificence of my future. What a future! A new world lay ready to my hand, newer than the world which the Spaniards found in the Western seas, for it was a fool's paradise that existed only in my imagination.

Alas! It soon faded and I returned once more to the reality of my position, under the wise guidance of Edward

Garnett, whom I met a few days later at my publisher's office. This great man has helped and influenced most of the important writers of his generation. To me his personality and friendship were of incalculable importance. There I was, like the innocent Huron of Voltaire, afloat in a crazy coracle on the sea of London literary life, surrounded by deadly rocks and yet without a thought for the dangers that surrounded me. Like a father he took me under his protection, handling me with the delicacy with which one handles a high-strung young colt, which the least mistake might make unfit for racing. It was the first time I had come in close contact with a cultured English gentleman. The calmness of his judgment, the subtlety of his intellect and the extraordinary nobility of his character were a glorious revelation to me, who had for years mingled almost entirely with rude and brutal types. So that I was only too willing that he should fashion the development of my literary talent in whatever way he pleased. Artistic beauty being the only thing of real importance in life to him, I became a fervent disciple of that religion. I abandoned at once all thought of making a "success" in life, of gaining fame or money. In a frenzy of enthusiasm I began to write *The Black Soul*, bringing the manuscript to Garnett page by page, angry when he threw some in the fire, delirious with joy when he said: "This is good." And as my interest in writing as an art increased, the idea of my marriage became more and more repellent. Finally, on the advice of Garnett, I left my garret and went to stay at a farmhouse in the country. There I wrote to my fiancée, saying that I was breaking off the engagement.

By return of post I received a long letter from her mother, a magnificent piece of vituperation, in which the venerable old lady said I was an insolent and ungrateful peasant. I had wormed my way into her house, toyed with the affections of her daughter, ruined her business, and then, as soon as I had found the means of escaping from my penury, I had broken off my engagement in the most offensive manner. "You have the characteristics of a low-born Irish peasant," she wrote. "Servile when you must, insolent when you may. Ye gods! That I should have harboured such vermin under my roof!" Attached to the letter was a bill, purporting to be the amount of money that I owed her. I have never made any attempt to pay this bill. The old lady died a few years later, the business was sold up to pay her debts and the daughter wrote to me several times for help. But I never answered her letters.

That is what the lean man, in the shabby trench-coat, with a revolver strapped between his shoulder-blades, had to say to me in the Luxembourg Gardens. He looked at me in horror and seemed to think that I had corrupted him. I? What I? Was it not he who had done so, and was I not now suffering from the result of his folly? That man was my youth and I was a shattered, disillusioned man of thirty-seven, looking with dry sorrow at the evil my youth had done.

"Oh, God!" I cried, covering my face with my hands. "Why must I suffer like this? I have never done evil intentionally. I have never taken pleasure in injuring a fellow human being, and yet my life has been strewn with the wreckage I have caused by my carelessness and folly.

Where is this girl whom I injured? If she appeared here before me now, would she find me more happy than she herself? What is the use of facing my conscience? I have gone too far. There is no hope of ever feeling right again."

Then I suddenly took a sombre delight in the hopelessness of my position. Away with the idea of reformation! I had thirty-seven pounds. I took out my wallet and counted them. Then I winked and looked about me, smiling in a cunning fashion.

IV

I GOT up and walked along the avenue, under the trees, feeling so elated that I wanted to sing. Enchanting visions passed before my mind, moving with the grace and sweetness of a love that assumes mortal shape through the intensity of its tenderness. I saw among them the ghost of my innocence rise on white wings from the hands of many devils who tried in vain to hold it. It soared swiftly into a dazzling place among the stars and left a trail of brightness when it vanished. Then I cried out:

"Sing no more of your contamination, but through love's ecstasy make music with your fancies in gentle, soothing peace. When the lark warbles in the misty morning air, his merry prattle brings out the lazy sun, and lo, the bleak fog is swept from the sky's blue face. A sick heart is most in need of laughter. And laughter breeds laughter. Beginning in a sweet image that the mind conceives, it floats through all the rivers of the blood, which it scours of bitterness. Why howl like a dog because you have experienced this and that and the other, which you think evil? Can any experience be evil to a poet? Is not all experience the rich meat and sensual wine of life on which he feeds? God gave you a hawk's wings and a hawk's far-seeing eye to prey upon the mice and sparrows of mediocrity. Not even a million sparrows are worth a falcon, for they lack the soaring beauty of his wings and his kingly eye."

I felt that I must find some person with whom to share this wild gaiety. Not a person that I knew, but some stranger to whom I would be a complete stranger. A woman preferably, as the personality of a woman is more receptive than that of a man and therefore she is a better companion when one is in the mood to give exuberantly. So I wandered about looking for one. As chance would have it, I did not have to wander very far. I was looking at the window of a book-shop in a little street off the Boulevard Saint Michel, when a woman came and stood beside me. At first I only noted the general appearance of her body, her full bust, her erect carriage, the way her hair curled on the nape of her strong neck, her fine grey hair and the smoothness of her tawny face. Then she looked at me and I felt drawn forcibly by the sadness of her eyes. I smiled and we began to talk.

"You look just as sad as I was a few minutes ago," I began.

"Yes," she said without any embarrassment, "I am sad. How did you know?"

"Your eyes. Is it just because you are lonely, or bored, or are you really sad?"

"What are you? An Englishman?"

"I was born in Ireland, just as you were born in America, but that is of no importance. When human beings are young, when they are smug with contentment, ignorantly self-assertive through the fanaticism born of gross ambition or greed, then the difference of race becomes important to them. Then an American looks with contempt on a Japanese or a Zulu, an Englishman despises an Italian and so forth. But people who through misfortune or old age have been purified of gross longings and reach a state of philosophic indifference to their environment, tend towards a true understanding of their common humanity. Have you ever noticed how difficult it is to tell the nationality of very old people? The shrivelled face of a very old American negress is exactly like, or almost like, the shrivelled face of a very old European queen; even like the shrivelled face of some very old New York society woman."

The woman stiffened and said:

"You are trying to be offensive. A negress like a white woman! What an absurd idea!"

I bowed and said gaily:

"I'm not trying to be offensive, but if you are sad, you must be really sad. Otherwise I shan't talk to you."

"I don't think I want you to."

"Oh, but you do. In any case I want to talk to you, and that is the important thing. I have something to tell you. I must tell somebody or do something foolish. The more appropriate the person to whom I tell it, the less foolish will be the outcome. And I think you are very appropriate. But you must be really humble."

"I think you are mad," she said.

"Of course I am mad, otherwise I would not have to talk to you. My wisdom of the moment is unlike that of the philosopher, for I am what I see instead of merely understanding it. And being what I see I am movement, and being movement I am mad. After all, what is madness but a failure to control the intensified activity of the imagination?"

The woman began to laugh and said:

"Well! In any case you are amusingly mad. I rather like you."

"Splendid," I cried. "Then we'll go and have lunch and you'll tell me why you are sad. Taxi!"

In the taxi she told me that she had just come from Switzerland and that she was trying to muster up courage to return home to New York.

"Does it require courage to return to New York?" I said. "I mean for an American? For me of course it would require courage to go there, for I was quite exhausted by my last visit to that extraordinary town. It is so beautiful that living there makes one violently intoxicated the whole time. But being American you should be used to it. Why don't you want to go back there?"

"That is a long story," she said. "I don't know whether I could tell you. And yet, you look sympathetic."

"Do you know why?"

"Why?"

"Because I am so much more unhappy than you could possibly be. Have you had children?"

"Yes, I have had two. I have two grown-up

daughters. Why do you ask? You say extraordinary things."

"Not really. A woman who has had children has fulfilled herself. After having fulfilled herself in that way, she has satisfied the most urgent craving of her being. But for me it is impossible to fulfil myself. There is an old proverb in my country which says: *Is geal le préachaun dubh a h-éinín féin.* That means that a raven thinks her little one is white; whiteness being symbolic of beauty. But I can see the flaws in the children of my imagination. I know that I could never produce one that would be one millionth part as beautiful as the child of my conception. That is the root of my unhappiness."

"What are you, then?" she said.

"Later, I shall tell you," I said. "First of all, you must drink red wine and tell me about *your* sadness. Here we are."

We sat opposite one another at a small table and then I could see that she must have been very beautiful in her youth; a purely physical beauty that lacked subtlety. The beauty of American women is like that. It reaches its perfection in the bodies of chorus girls, and when it is allied to wit, the wit is comic. It lacks the elegant sharpness which ennobles the beauty of great European whores. Only great whores are really beautiful, for true beauty is a combination of good and evil. In the beauty of motherhood there is only good. This woman's beauty had been that of a young mother rather than that of a young whore, hising up the silky nakedness of her lissom thighs before the lecherous gloating of old men. And yet, she was now approaching middle age, without having learnt to be content with her virtue being its own reward. The sacred vessel of her womb had twice performed the miracle of life. Now its door was closed and the God of life in her had laid down his wand, but instead of bowing her head in gratitude for what she had received, she longed for youth and the ecstasy of love. Sombre autumn had died her hair to the likeness of pale, wintry death and her limbs had lost their comeliness. But her eyes were wanton, tell-tale gossips of the lust that burned within her.

"Drink," I said to her, " and forgive me for not drinking. I don't need wine. At this moment it would make my mind over-reach itself."

At first she refused to drink alone, but suddenly she took up a glass and drank greedily, like a person ashamed of showing his excessive hunger. Then she began to talk.

"I dare say I am a fool to talk to you, a stranger, about myself," she said, "but I feel that I must talk to somebody. In any case, I have made such a fool of myself that it doesn't matter any more."

"On the contrary," I said, "you are probably just beginning to learn how to live. In order to live as one should, one should make a fool of oneself. I bet that you are unhappy simply because you didn't make a fool of yourself when you were young. In that way, at least, I am happier than you. All my life I have eagerly and willingly and unrepentantly made a fool of myself."

"I don't understand you," she said. "What do you mean?"

"Tell me first why you are unhappy."

"Because I loved somebody and he turned out to be a rotter."

"When did you love this man? Recently, or before you were married?"

"Recently. I just left him in Switzerland."

"You didn't love your husband then?"

"Oh, I don't know. I suppose I did in a way. I married when I was eighteen. I didn't know much about love then. I suppose I really married him because it was a good match and we were fond of one another."

"And then?"

"Oh, we were as happy as most people. He was very successful. We were rich and we had two beautiful children. There wasn't much time to think of other things."

"What other things?"

"Oh, I don't know. Love, I suppose. I really had a horror of those things. In America we thought that sort of thing was wicked. But when the children grew up and Charles had got old, he was much older than I was, I began to feel so terribly lonely. You know, as if there were something I hadn't done. There are so many women in America like that. The dangerous age they call it, and they are quite right. To escape from this loneliness I used to attend lectures and try to interest myself in art, but I really didn't know anything about it. I couldn't learn, although I loved it so much. I wanted to understand so much how to appreciate beautiful things. That's how I met this man. He was a painter. He lived in Greenwich Village in New York and he was starving.

I thought he was a genius and I fell in love with him. He pretended to be in love with me too, so I took him to Switzerland with me. There I soon found out what he really was. He got ten thousand dollars out of me and then ran off to Hungary with a young Viennese girl."

"He was quite right," I said.

"Oh!" she said. "How can you be so cruel?"

"Well, wouldn't it be far greater cruelty on your part to keep this young man, who no longer loved you, in your bed?"

"How crude you are suddenly! I thought you were so sympathetic."

"I have no sympathy with people who bewail the price they have paid for love."

"I'm not bewailing the price I paid, but he might have been honest with me. And it was all the money I had left. I am now penniless. My husband went bankrupt in this crash on Wall Street. He threw himself from the twenty-second story of a building."

"Good Lord! What was he? I mean . . ."

"A banker."

"I see. And now you . . ."

"I don't know what to do."

"Neither do I, if you mean that you don't know how to make enough money in order to live without having to think about the struggle for bread. But are you really penniless? Forgive my being personal, but is that ring a genuine black pearl, or is it an imitation?"

"It's genuine," she said, stiffening as she had done when I compared an old negress to an old New York society woman. "I have never worn anything artificial."

"At that rate, it's worth a few hundred pounds. Good Lord! I feel almost certain that, if you sold everything of value you possess, you would quite likely have a thousand pounds. Eh?"

She looked at me in astonishment and some fear, as I was leaning across the table and speaking with great intensity in order to hypnotize her into my own state of feeling.

"Tell me," I said. "Is it true or is not true that you could realize a thousand pounds if you sold all you possess?"

"I dare say I could raise that sum," she said, "if I sold everything."

"Ha! ha!" I cried. "See what a humbug you are. If I had a thousand pounds and if I were as free of responsibility as you are, how lucky I would consider myself! Are your daughters in any way dependent on you?"

"That's the worst of it. They have just left college and God only knows what's going to happen to them. They were to go on a world trip with their father. It's too awful. I daren't face them, but I must."

"Are they healthy?"

"Oh, yes. Both strong, healthy girls."

"Are they good looking?"

"They are both beautiful. Marion in particular."

"Then forget about them. Let them look after themselves. If the factories in America are closed, they have still the oldest profession in the world to provide them with a living, if they are clever enough. If they are not clever enough to sell themselves, they are not worth helping. It is natural for a mother to drive away her young when it is fanged or fully fledged and thus equipped to prey on other forms of life. Learn, you foolish woman, that life is an interminable process of one form of life preying on another, from the cow that destroys life in the blade of grass, to the lion that leaps upon a stag in the African forest. Aye! And to your dead husband, who, in his lair on Wall Street, more savage and merciless than any lion, tracked down his prey. Now your male is dead, and if you are wise you'll keep away from the country where he hunted. Shall I tell you what to do?"

By now she was staring at me, fascinated like a rabbit crouched before a circling stoat. She nodded and raised to her lips the glass I had refilled. I waited until she had drained it. Her eyes did not leave mine, even while she drank. Now they had a strange expression. They were no longer sad. "The dream" had taken hold. She had already forgotten the pain of this other "dream," impersonated in the man who had gone into Hungary with a young Viennese girl. Now her eyes were drunk; not with wine alone but with lust. A used but unsated woman fashioning a new maidenhead in the heat of her Indian summer.

"There is an island off the west coast of Ireland," I whispered, "where I was born. Sell everything you have got and go there. With one thousand pounds you will be able to make yourself secure there against want for the rest of your life. Let me tell you about it. Right on the highest point of the island there is an old watchtower. You can rent this tower for a few pounds a year. For one hundred pounds you can have it repaired and furnished simply. It stands within an enclosure of about one acre of land. There is a high wall around this land, making good shelter against the storms of winter. So that it is a good place to grow all kinds of vegetables and even fruit like gooseberries and currants. There would be, besides, enough grass and briars at one end to feed a goat or two. There is a shed where you could keep two pigs. These you could feed easily on your excess vegetables, as well as a dozen or so of hens. About half a mile away, on the north coast of the island, there is a tiny cove, where you could keep a small boat. You could learn to row this boat and fish in it. With a tram net and a lobster pot, you could get lobsters, cray-fish, pollock, rock-fish, and then if you became handy with a fishing-line and hook, you could also get mackerel and bream. On the shore there is an abundance of periwinkles, crabs, mussels, cockles, sand-herrings, shrimps and sea-mosses of various kinds that are most excellent for their medicinal qualities. All this you could enjoy without having to buy or sell, without expenditure of money except for the initial outlay on the purchase of tools, seeds and the animals. You could live independent of society, maintaining yourself by your own labour. If you wanted luxuries, like tea, sugar, flour and paraffin to make light, I have no doubt but that the sale of one pig would be sufficient to purchase them all. The other pig, of course, you could slaughter and turn into bacon. As also you could eat the hens when they ceased to lay and the young cockerels from each clutch of chicks. Do you see?"

She stared at me in a hostile way. The expression of eager lust had changed to a malicious envy.

"I don't understand," she said in a sour tone.

Suddenly, the wine she had drunk turned sour in her.

"You don't understand," I cried, "no more than you could understand the lectures you attended, or the dreams of the young man you followed from New York to Switzerland. Like your husband, you are a beast of prey. So you don't understand when I suggest your becoming the humble servant of your own needs. Mark you, there are some beings who are worthy of being served, worthy of being given food and drink and shelter and reverence, in order that humanity may benefit from the flowering of their intellects. But you are not one of them. Neither was your husband. You both belong to those who serve. He threw himself from the twenty-second story of a building when he was cornered. And you, when you tried to prey on the virility and imagination of a young painter, were routed by a young Viennese girl. And now you think that the world is cruel to you. But what have you to give the world? Nothing but the decaying mask of a beauty that has withered. For shame, woman."

She began to tremble, and then I reached across the table and took her by the hand.

"Forgive me," I said. "Don't think I am cruel, but I said you must be humble. If you are humble enough, then 'the slings and arrows of outrageous fortune' will ennoble you instead of casting you down. Listen to me. I said I am unhappier than you, because I am capable of more unhappiness. I am a writer, and when the fiery ecstasy was young in me, I felt that I could storm the highest heavens with my songs. But like a puny bird, who dares the ocean's width in search of warmth at the fall of winter, my tired wings soon forced me to drop exhausted on a ship returning to the cold that I had left. I never reached heaven. Shall I tell you about it?"

The woman got to her feet and said:

"I think I must be going."

I stared at her intently for some time and then I realized definitely that I had made a mistake. What she wanted was not mine to give. Bah! Contamination!

"She is a mouse that scratches in dusty cellars, a sparrow from the gutter of a city slum, and I am a sick hawk. I cannot eat."

I left her, took a cab and drove to a cinema, in order to get over the irritation caused by the American woman. I settled myself comfortably and tried to become interested in the film, but was unable to do so. In spite of myself, my eyes wandered away from the screen, they became fixed, and I saw the watch-tower of which I had spoken to the woman. Indeed, I had offered her my own retreat, but of course I knew she would not act on my advice. And in any case, I was in doubt whether it was my own retreat. If it were, want of money would not keep me away from it. Or was it want of humility?

Now I remembered how I went back there after the publication of my novel, *The Black Soul*, had persuaded me that I could never hope to carry the fortress of literature by assault. That was the song with which I hoped to storm the highest heavens, but it was received instead by a storm of the most violently adverse criticism. Edward Garnett wrote to me saying that the critics had killed the book for ten years. I felt that they had killed me with it, and my childish vanity drove me into a frenzy of rage. I wrote to him saying that these critics did not have sufficient blood in them to contract syphilis, and then I got on the train for the Aran Islands, swearing that I would never leave it again.

In Galway I met my sister. At that time she was very ill, but in my excitement at returning home I did not notice it. On the boat coming from Galway to the islands, she told me how difficult things were for her at home, how father was alone and doting. Whose father? What? I walked up and down the deck of the boat, crying out as each headland came into view. When the grey mass of the islands rose suddenly from the white-capped sea, I felt that this was indeed the promised land to which I had returned. All the people on the boat looked askance at me, for I had already become a damned soul in their eyes. But I was indifferent to them also and I stood apart, opening my mouth, so that the wild sea wind could rush freely into my lungs, to blow away the rank air of cities. And then we reached the shore.

Immediately, I felt an alien among the people who stood on the pier. They spoke to me and shook me by the hand, but there was fear in their eyes. Had it been hatred, I would not have felt an alien; but this mute fear was deeper than hatred and unapproachable. One could not speak to it, haul it out from the soul and hold it up for examination. It was like a shameful vice which one does not acknowledge even to one's conscience. I walked up the pier with my sister, glancing shyly, with a timid lover's eyes, at the familiar rocks, fields, houses and at the same time feeling all round me these watching eyes and the whispered pity for one who had been a kinsman and had become contaminated. With what?

The madness of prophecy, no less. This is the greatest sin in the eyes of the herd. And when one of the herd becomes gifted with this madness, he at once becomes an object of fear for the rest. In strong and rich societies he is tolerated as an amusing outcast; but in a weak and poor herd, the fear is much greater, sometimes leading to expulsion and death. A criminal! To sing of beauty should be such a lovely thing.

Even my sister had the same fear in her eyes, but she was too near my blood to show it; and I, even though I felt that fear, was too exalted to be affected by it on the surface. Yet I was glad when we got to the hotel and were alone. And then we walked west to see my father. It was an afternoon in March and Spring was already in the air. The earth was turning green. It imparted its fever to me. And yet, I could not enjoy this fever because of my sister who gave it a different meaning. To her it was a manifestation of God's bounty, showing His love for men, softening their hearts and making them repent of their sins, in order to win a place in Paradise, where they could sing of beauty for all eternity. But I wanted to sing then, at that very moment; to seize the people who passed by the bosom and shout at them: "Come, brothers and sisters, listen to the call of Spring and make merry while the blood is still warm in your veins. Soon the day will come when your blood will cease to flow and worms shall devour your flesh, which can now feel the delights of tender passion."

And then, seeing that even my sister whom I loved had become alien to me, I knew that it was no use my fleeing to this island that had given me birth. These people were even more hostile to me than the critics who had denounced my book. They were all, both the critics and these people among whom I was born, of the common herd, slaveling serfs who grovelled before false gods; gods in their own liking; toy monsters without any noble attribute. A pride like Lucifer's buoyed me up to the sombre loneliness of universal understanding; the pride of Socrates when the hemlock moistened his doomed tongue and his wit was martyred by the envious mob of Athens. "Father, forgive them for they know not what they do." Forgive them not, I say, but lash their slavish backs and make them minister unto your wants. Wherever you see an ignorant eye spit on it; for it has committed the sin against the Holy Ghost by looking into yours, its master's eye.

It was already dusk when we came to our village. With horror I saw the house where I was born, falling rapidly into ruins. The little garden in front was overgrown with weeds. The roof of the outhouse was sagging in the middle. Grass was growing through the thatch. And within the house itself there was the same air of desolation. But more desolate than the house and its surroundings was my father himself, that doddering old man who shook hands with me and mumbled half-articulate words without knowing me.

Could this shapeless man be the handsome young lover about whom I had heard at my mother's knee in childhood? His eyes were sunk deeply in their bony sockets. One was almost blind and colourless. The lids were naked and red. The other eye still looked piercing. It seemed to stand apart from its fellow, giving the whole face a startling appearance. It was the only thing alive in the shrivelled face. The white beard was unkempt. The foolish old man had cut it with a pair of scissors, hacking a piece here and there. His mouth had sunk as deeply as his eyes. When he opened it to speak, I could see that he had lost all his teeth except one, which was loose and bobbed about as the palsied tongue struck against it, forming the stuttered words. The forehead was strangely white and the great scar on the right temple looked new; as if it were going to bleed afresh. On the long skull the white hair was like a wig, limp and close-lying and unnatural. The long, straight nose was the only feature that retained the noble beauty which had been the admiration of my childhood.

When I entered the house he came forward eagerly to meet me, his hat in his hand, smiling and bowing. When he tried to bow, he curtsied like a woman. There was no strength in his hand. The fingers had curved inwards on the palm, so that it was impossible to grip the hand in the ordinary way. His body seemed to have shrunk to half its size. In its shabby suit of frieze it was unrecognizable, so withered and uncertain of movement.

"Ho!" he cried in a jovial tone. "This is a great honour. Have you come far? You are very welcome. Stay for a month. But perhaps your aeroplane is waiting."

"Oh, father, don't you know who it is?" my sister said.

"Eh?" he said, staring at her in a queer way. "Of

course I do. Do you think I don't know how to re
people properly in my own house?"

Suddenly he grew very excited and shook his fist at some unknown enemies.

"I'll show them all," he cried fiercely, "that I am still on my feet, the scoundrels."

He looked at me cunningly and whispered:

"They are trying to murder me. They steal everything I have. I do have to be on my guard night and day."

Then he seemed to lose all interest in me. He began to mumble to himself. He picked up a short stick, buttoned his jacket and prepared to leave the house.

"Where are you going, father?" my sister said.

"Eh?" he said. "Isn't this young man the jobber? I must show him the heifer, I suppose, if he wants to see her. It's a bit too early in the year yet, but she is in fine condition."

My sister burst into tears.

"He has been like this since he had the stroke last summer," she said. "It's so hard."

Then I realized for the first time how she must have suffered all these months, coming from the village each evening after finishing work in her school. Eight miles each evening in the depth of winter to tend an old man who had occasional lapses into idiocy. I realized how awful it must have been for her to come into this desolate house, almost naked of furniture, on a dark, stormy winter's evening, to find the old man sitting by the hearth, shaking his stick at imaginary enemies; this hearth that had once been merry with the laughter of many children, sitting around their mother, who told them stories. All gone but herself; dead or scattered over the earth. And worse than death, this doting father, whose stern nature had always seemed to be immune from influence by any emotion, either of pain or of joy. Now a babbling dotard, furious with insane fancies, kept alive only by some savage courage that resisted death.

"Cheer up," I cried. "I'll look after him now. Come along. Let's see the heifer."

"Very well, sir," he said cheerfully. "Although I warn you that I'm not inclined to sell."

I laughed and my sister seemed affected by my laughter, for she stopped crying and said she would get a meal ready before we came back. Then I set off with my father. As soon as we were away from the house he became very confidential and said in a cunning whisper:

"She is the worst of them."

"Who?" I said.

"That woman there in the house. There isn't a day but she comes spying on me. Not only that, but she hires the others to come and torment me. They stole a cup yesterday while I was at the shore. Last week they took a jug off the dressers."

Then he suddenly halted in the road, looked at me closely and said:

"Which of them are you? I had two and they both went away. I am a lonely man. Are you Tom?"

"No," I said. "He is in America."

"Ha!" he said, continuing to walk. "Your mother would be glad to see you, but she is gone, Lord have mercy on her. I was married to your mother fifty years, but the year she is dead is longer than the fifty. I don't know what I'm waiting for. Nor would I wait only . . ."

Again he halted and threatened the air with his stick. "They want to get rid of me," he cried fiercely, " but I'll see them all in their graves."

With this outburst he again lapsed into senile idiocy. He talked to me as to a stranger and his manner was gay. Now it was dusk and we had descended into the deep valley below the village. All along the semi-circle of low cliffs that ringed this valley birds were twittering softly in their shelters. There was hardly any wind. There was a ghostly silence except for the soft twittering of the birds. I felt terribly lonely and yet exalted. We were following a path through the stony fields to the heifer. Every inch of the ground was familiar to me, associated with memories of my childhood, memories that kept rushing into my mind. I wanted to cry like my sister, and at the same time, even stronger than this lonely sadness, a great joy made me want to kneel and kiss the earth. I trembled as I walked beside my father, who had now become a symbol of something too holy for my human understanding. Can one look on God in His nakedness? Bow your head, sinner. Night is falling and the earth holds out her arms.

"Now," I thought, "I am saved. I have seen the world and found it wanting. Here is peace. Here suffering is holy and happiness is being in harmony with nature. Think no more."

We climbed over a stone wall into a small round field, where I had once watched a mare drop a foal. How amazed I was to see its bag burst as it touched the sward! Then the foal slipped out on to the grass, on which its new-born body left a rime. And also, at dawn one Spring morning, I helped a sheep give birth to a lamb. Dawn and birth and Spring! Now it was night, and my father, trembling with old age, went up to the red heifer and spoke softly to her. She stretched out her head and made a low, crooning sound. He scratched her head between the horns. Then he began to praise her beauty, laying his stick along her back and showing me how her red hair curled on her spine.

"She'll be a champion," he said. "She'd be a champion now, only for a chill she got in January."

Then we returned to the house. On the road we met a man coming home from milking his cow. The three of us leaned over the fence and we began to talk. This man spoke of my father as if he were a child, and I found this strange; for in the old days people were afraid to speak in my father's presence. But I was glad that this man spoke to me as to a kinsman. In his voice was the whispered tenderness of a person speaking to one of his blood of intimate things. There was none of the fear which I noticed in the eyes of the people on the pier. Here I was at home, in my own village, among my own people. I was no longer an outcast. Holy earth.

"It was I found him in the field," the man said. "It was last August, or it might be July. He was cutting briars and the sun all at once got the better of him. He fell down with the reaping hook in his hand. I was riding west on my horse when I noticed him lying there between two bushes. I ran down to him and turned him on his back. There was a little froth on his lips and I thought he was dead. I took him home on the horse, but he was on his feet again after a few days. It would have killed another man. He has the strength of a lion."

"God spare your health," I said.

"May God look down on us!" he said. "May He forget the evil we do and only remember the good! What is there worth having except the love of neighbours? To help one another as best we can and to live at peace. Even the mighty of the earth can do no more, and if we do that, God does the rest. We are poor, but sure the poor can love one another, and what else is there?"

We ate the meal my sister had prepared and then the old man went to bed. My sister and myself returned to the hotel. I could not stay with my father as there was only one bed in the house. In any case he did not wish me to stay, insisting that I had an aeroplane waiting for me and that I must hurry in order to catch it. On the way back to the hotel I could feel the trembling of my sister's body. But we could not bare our souls to one another. In the strange way that sensitive people find it more difficult to talk to those they love about intimate things than to strangers, we were silent about our sorrow and only spoke of trivial things. And then, next morning I returned to my father. I found him in his normal senses and so charming that it was difficult to believe he had been an idiot on the previous evening. I asked him would he like me to stay in the house with him and look after him.

"Pooh!" he said. "Why would you stay here?

There is nothing here for you. Go your road. Do you need money? If you do, I have some. Not much, but I have some. Eh? Did I ever tell you the story about the blind man that was brought looking for a wife to Connemara at dead of night?"

I spent the day walking about the cliffs, trying to make up my mind what to do. And I felt terribly ashamed, because I knew that my mind was already made up and that I would not stay. Every moment of life there would be like a wound. And so it happened. Three days later I fled back to Dublin.

The boat was leaving for the mainland before dawn. I got up in the middle of the night, packed my bag and went into my sister's room at the hotel. She was lying awake.

"I am going," I said.

"God bless you," she said, stroking my face with her thin, nervous hand.

The dawn was very rough and the crew of the boat were in doubt about being able to make the crossing; but I urged them to set forth, and at length they agreed to do so. As soon as we left the harbour the wind screamed about us and the light boat heaved about on the rolling waves like a cork.

"Where was I going?"

I asked this question in quite a loud voice, and the people who sat near me in the cinema looked at me in astonishment. Somebody asked me to keep silent. I was on the point of retorting angrily, but instead I got to my feet and hurried out into the street. Again I thought I was going to fall down, but I made a great effort and regained control of myself. Then I returned to my hotel, went to bed and slept soundly until nine o'clock the following morning.

## V

My nerves were in much better condition on awaking. Abstinence from tobacco and alcohol was beginning to have its effect. I jumped out of my bed, feeling extremely high spirited. My throat did not feel sore. My mind was calm, and as I dressed I began to make plans for the work I was to do on getting to Brittany. Then I went once more to the police about my typewriter. Alas! There was no sign of it.

"We'll communicate with you," they said, "when it turns up."

Again I left the place in a quandary. Now what was I to do? I could not stay in Paris for ever waiting for the recovery of the wretched typewriter. The city irritated me and I would be sure to get into trouble after a few days. In any case, it was bad for me, in my present nervous state, to mope about having fits of remorse. I needed fresh air.

"Devil take the typewriter," I cried. "I'm leaving this evening. But what am I to do in the meantime?"

I bought a copy of *Paris Midi* from a lad at a street corner. Ha! It was the day of the Grand Prix. At once a lump came into my throat. Why not go to it? Angrily I began to reason with this desire, urging that it would be supreme folly, just as I was setting out to get rid of my vicious habits and turn over a new leaf. A mania for horse-racing had been one of the many causes of getting me into my present position. Away with it!

"Not on any account," I said to myself. "I shan't set foot in Saint Cloud to-day. To hell with racing!"

I dropped the paper on the pavement and walked away, but impelled by some unconscious force I came back again and picked it up. Then I turned the pages feverishly until I came to the race programme.

"No harm in looking at the runners in any case," I said to myself. "It will pass the time for an hour."

I sat down in front of a café, ordered some Vichy water and began to study the probable runners for the big race. Goyescas was one of the fancied candidates. Excitedly, I recalled the race for the Eclipse Stakes at Sandown two years previously. I had gone down with an American named Evans, who kept telling me that he had a good tip for a horse called Caerleon. I told him that Caerleon could not win the race if he got a five furlong start, that Goyescas was a certainty and that he would win in a canter. I lost Evans in the ring before the big race. Then I went up on the stand to watch it. I had put all the money I had on Goyescas. It was raining and I had no field-glasses. The horses were a blur as they ran down the far side of the course. Then they came across and turned into the straight. A woman beside me said that Goyescas was lying in a good position. Then somebody shouted that the favourite would win in a canter. I began to tremble with excitement. They came nearer and I picked out the colours of my horse. It shot into the lead and it looked all over a winner, when suddenly it was challenged on the rails. By what? Lord Derby's colours, somebody said. By God! It was Caerleon, with Weston riding in a frenzy. He came alongside Goyescas and then got his head in front. Goyescas began to jerk his head upwards and I knew I had lost. I went into the ring and found Evans sitting on the concrete, indifferent to the rain, his overcoat unbuttoned, bareheaded, with a bundle of bookmaker's tickets in his hand. He had won hundreds of pounds at thirty-three to one.

And now I came across Goyescas once more. What was the meaning of it? Had I lost my typewriter and been delayed in Paris in order that I might " pull off a coup " on this horse? But how could I do so with thirty-five pounds, considering that the horse would probably be at a very short price on the tote? Not enough, at least, to install myself in that watch-tower and become independent of society. Again I threw down the paper and decided to have nothing to do with the business. But the fascination was too strong. I began to revel in the dream of winning a great deal of money Once more I examined the programme. In the first race I saw an animal called Why Worry II. It seemed an obvious pointer. Indeed! Why worry? Now all was clear. I would go to the races, win an enormous sum and clear myself of all cause for worry.

There are very few forms of intoxication known to man more delirious than the intoxication of gambling. Indeed, it is very questionable whether any intoxication is equal to it, for it is a state of mind which merely requires the acquiescence of the will in order to attain complete fruition. And gambling on race-horses is, to my mind, superior to any other form. Betting on cards, or on the spin of a wheel, is an inferior and base form of gambling. Once at the Casino Municipal in Nice, I won twenty-seven thousand francs in twenty minutes at Boule; and I still remember how base and sordid the transaction seemed to me. How unclean I felt standing at that sombre table among all the mean, shrivelled faces that lined the board! There the vice of greed stood triumphant and unashamed, while beyond, in a great room, his companion lechery had marshalled a horde of harlots to devour the profits of the winners, or to console the losers. But in gambling on race-horses the vice is purified by participation in a noble sport, which has been rightly called "the sport of kings."

Is there anyone who can stand among a Derby crowd on the hill at Epsom and remain unmoved by the stupendous enthusiasm when the public fancy races past the post a winner? Or at Aintree, when the National field is lined up at the start and a hush falls on the tense multitude, and then the great roar, "They're off," drowns the thunder of the parting hooves? When I think of all the moments of glorious living that racing has given me, a lump comes into my throat. Here I see a horse being led, at a distance, across the windswept Curragh of Kildare. The young colt whinnies and the breeze lifts a corner of its mane. Or again, at the Curragh, I see four men dancing with joined hands on the top of the stand, after the gallant but ill-fated West Indies had won the Guineas. I see Orwell come with a great rush from the

Dip at Newmarket and race past the swerving Dastur. I see the crowd standing on the stone walls at Punchestown, shouting and waving their sticks. But enough . . .

I made my way at once to Saint Cloud, where I arrived about noon. What a difference there is between a French race-course and a race-course in any part of these islands! Here the important thing is the horse. Everything is arranged for its comfort and its dominance of the meeting. In France the horse is merely an important actor in the entertainment offered to the spectator. But it is the spectator who dominates. In France a race-meeting is rather like an open-air theatrical show; whereas with us it has some of the grimness of a number of strong men on horseback going out on a cold day to kill a small fox. But enough . . . enough . . . I am on the point of becoming offensive.

Having had lunch, I changed my money into francs and prepared for the struggle with fortune. All told I had two thousand five hundred francs. Of this sum I decided to invest a thousand on Why Worry II. I would skip the second race in which I fancied nothing, put a hundred on Pick Up in the third and plunge on Goyescas in the Grand Prix. Then I sat under a tree near the paddock to wait for the tote to open business on the first race. The crowd was beginning to pour on to the course and there was a babble of conversation. There were numbers of pretty women in magnificent frocks, old men with decorations and eye-glasses, gangs of officials rushing about, gesticulating, all the gorgeous tumult and expectancy that presages the commencement of a meeting. The excitement was too strong for my reliance on my "hunch." I felt that they were all bound to lose, and in any case, even if they won . . .

Suddenly I realized that there was a man sitting beside me on the bench. Indeed he had already spoken to me. At first I did not understand what he had said and I listened, waiting for him to repeat it. I dared not look at him. For a long time he remained silent and then again he spoke.

"Don't pretend you have forgotten me, or that it's possible for you to forget her," he said in a solemn tone.

I shuddered and said:

"You swine, you choose a nice moment to remind me of her. In any case, she's your business not mine."

"Quite so," he said, "but I'm your business. You can't get rid of me. Let me tell you the truth."

"I don't want to hear anything just now," I cried angrily. "Can't you leave me alone? I want to make some money."

"And then?"

"If I make enough," I answered, "it will solve her problem. I'll give it to her. All of it. All, I tell you."

"I doubt it very much," he said. "If you made a lot of money you would probably spend it all at once, just as you did when you won twenty-seven thousand francs at Nice. The following morning you had ten francs and you had to borrow your fare back to Marseilles."

"That is true," I said, "but at that time I didn't really want the money. I had met on the train coming from Marseilles a strange Irishman, an oldish judge who was travelling with a beautiful Russian woman. It was the excitement of meeting them, especially the strangeness of the Irishman, which made me go into the casino to gamble, and then after coming out I joined up with that gang of young people who were celebrating the carnival and we went into an underground cabaret."

"All that is beside the point," he said gloomily. "I cannot disassociate myself from you, no more than you can get rid of her. As Hauser said, you'll never be able to do it."

"That is quite true. But what do you want?"

"I want you to humble yourself."

"That I could never do, even if I wanted to do so. I have always stood alone, even when I loved her. What I suffer on her account, in my soul, is what you make me suffer. You are a paltry fellow. It is only when I am you that I am ashamed of myself. Marriage means nothing to me as an artist, nor women either, except as living phenomena whose actions and emotions I examine and try to understand, since they are a living part of the material I use in my work. Just now a weasel is more important to me than any woman. A weasel I saw last year in Aran looking over a stone wall that surrounds a sally garden. How beautiful its throat looked and the line of its supple body. It had its head upraised and it was smelling the air. It smelt me, got startled and then glided away so quickly that my staring eyes could still see it peering over the fence after it had gone."

"If she means less to you than your weasel, why do you bother about her? Why must you try to make a lot of money in order to get rid of her problem, as you call it?"

75

This seemed so true that I could not find a reasonable answer for it. Then the man continued:

"You have always been able to find a plausible excuse for your folly. Why are you silent now?"

"Begone," I said. "You are just the link between me and mediocrity. You are the weakness in my nature that has made me a prey to women. You always had a sentimental craving for being in love and being loved and cared for and protected against life. But I don't want any protection."

"You say that now, but when you are ill you whinge."

"It's not I who whinge but you. I remember when I had a nervous breakdown and I arrived in Dublin penniless, without friends, I relied on myself for help."

"That's untrue. It was Edward Garnett who helped you."

"I know that, but I am referring to spiritual help. I realized, when I lay awake night after night, unable to sleep in spite of the drugs I was given, that when a man is bolt upright against annihilation he stands so far apart from other beings that he can get no assistance from them. Ha! ha! At that time you were powerless to interfere with the free functioning of my intellect. You moaned and blabbed about imaginary diseases, but I just lay in bed at night analysing your moaning. You even tried to make me afraid of God, but when the doctor came, perhaps at three o'clock in the morning, in answer to your hysterical calls for help, I enjoyed talking to him about the various symptoms of your neurasthenic cowardice. After all, you are useful to me. In you I can study the shabbiness of human nature, while in myself I can study its . . ."

"Its insanity," he whispered.

"Eh?" I cried, looking towards him for the first time.

It was after all only a small, fat American with horn-rimmed glasses who was asking me where he could buy a race-card. I told him and walked away, feeling certain that he had heard me talking to the imaginary man. I looked back. Apparently he had heard nothing, for he too was walking away, his hand to his forehead to shield his eyes from the brilliant sunlight, going towards the place I had indicated. Then I had not been talking aloud. Was it an hallucination? The thought was agonizing. I found another bench and sat down. It was very difficult to subdue the apprehensions that crowded on me. It was useless trying to steer my mind towards the business that I had in hand, even though I conjured up the most fantastic outcome of it, the winning of a sum so enormous that I could buy, not only the watch-tower, but the whole island, and repair, by immense gifts, all the damage I had ever committed. "Conscience," I cried, "is but a word that cowards use, devis'd at first to keep the strong in awe." Indeed! Was Shakespeare not making an excuse for himself when he put those words in the mouth of Richard, the hunchback? No, no. There it stood, my conscience, not a word that cowards use to keep the strong in awe, but a means of escape through pity and humility from the folly of callousness.

And whence did this hallucination come? Where

did it originate? Was it that night at Langemarck in September 1917? If so, I was not myself to blame, but an experience that had been stronger than my physical powers. It might be so. And yet I had always thought that I had been stronger than that experience. Now, however, the contrary seemed obvious. I saw it thus.

I was guiding the transport officer from the canal at Boesinghe to the position held by our company in the front line. Night had fallen and it was very difficult to find the road, when suddenly the Germans started firing with their artillery on a party of men who were bringing up supplies on trucks along a light railway. The transport officer and myself were caught in this barrage. We took refuge in a hole with two soldiers who had been working on the trucks. One of these kept moaning. He had been wounded somewhere. As he seemed to be badly wounded, the transport officer told me to carry him to the field-dressing station. I hauled him out of the hole and moved away to the left, in the direction they had pointed out to me. The shells were falling very heavily, and we stumbled over a dead man whose head had been blown away. The wounded man got into a panic and accused me of trying to kill him. He wanted to lie down in a hole until the firing stopped. I got very angry with him, because I could now see that he was not badly wounded at all, being merely hit somewhere in the shoulder; so I bundled him along as quickly as I could. We got to the shelter. I threw him among the other wounded and hurried back to the hole where I had left the transport officer. There was nobody there.

It was very dark and I didn't know what to do, as I

had completely lost my bearing. The artillery fire was becoming more intense. Machine-gun and rifle fire now added to the uproar. I heard shouting in front. I hurried towards the shouting and soon came on two men who were taking boxes from a truck that had been struck by a shell. They mumbled something about a German counter-attack and asked me to give them a hand. We hauled several boxes and bags of rations into a hole near the railway track which had been torn by the shells. One of the boxes had been broken. It contained bottles of whisky and stout. One of the men knocked off the head of a whisky bottle against the butt of his rifle. "If I'm going to be wiped out," he said, "let me die drunk." He began to drink from the torn neck of the bottle. I asked them had they seen the transport officer. Neither of them answered me. Suddenly a platoon of men advanced into view close on our right. The shells were bursting so thickly that their stooping bodies stood out brightly against the skyline. An officer with a revolver in his hand advanced in front shouting and swearing. The man handed me the whisky bottle and I put it to my head, at the same time watching the havoc of the enemy's fire among the stooping bodies of the advancing guardsmen. Somebody shouted: "Come on, the Irish." I handed back the bottle and continued to stare in a fascinated way at the falling men. Where were they going? Should I rush into action with them? And then, just as the man was again handing me the bottle for another drink, a roar and a flash enveloped me. A shell had fallen in our hole killing the two men with whom I was drinking.

The next thing I remember was sitting in a hole opposite a man who was bleeding to death, because his right arm had been shot away above the elbow. Two men were trying to bandage it, but it was very dark and the man would not keep still, but kept tossing about the stump of his arm and saying: "Jesus, Mary and Joseph, I offer you up my heart and soul." I began to laugh, and then I shouted as loud as I could: "Come on, the Irish." One of the men who were doing the bandaging turned around and said: "Keep quiet, you little bastard." Then he struck me in the face with the flat of his hand, which was dripping with blood from the other man's arm. "He's f——d," I heard a voice say, "no use wasting time on him. Let's take this other lad along." I struggled with them, but soon I became exhausted and they led me to the dressing-station where I had left the other wounded man a few minutes previously. I remember seeing a doctor stooping over a man whose stomach was wide open, and then somebody said: "What's the matter with you, mate? This part of you?" He picked a piece of mangled flesh from my tunic. Then I remember vaguely being in an ambulance bumping along a road where shells were falling. Afterwards things became more and more vague. It became difficult to speak, although I was continually conscious of having something very important to say and being unable to say it. Even when I tried to communicate seriously with those who were in charge of me, they refused to listen. Instead they treated me as if I were a child or an idiot. I remained for a long time somewhere lying on a stretcher-bed and then I was put in a train, lying opposite a man who was blind and who kept moaning the whole time that he would never again see his wife's hair. "It's so lovely," he said, "in the firelight. Last time home on leave we sat by the fire and I knew I'd never see her again. Oh, Christ! Won't somebody put me out of pain?" And then I was put into bed somewhere in the middle of the night.

It was there I regained complete consciousness, but only for a minute or even less. Suddenly I became aware that a woman in white was leaning over my cot. It was the perfume of her hair and the fragrance of her body that made me aware of her. I had been lying with my eyes closed, and when I opened my eyes in response to her fragrance, I saw her face close to mine. I thought it was my sister and that I had been having a nightmare, or perhaps it was the cold with which I was in bed when my sister came into the room and said war had been declared. That time I had jumped out of bed and cheered, wild with excitement. But now I put up my arms and caught this nurse by the shoulders and whispered to her: "Oh, where have I been? Why didn't you come for me before?"

And then, to my horror, I saw that her face was not my sister's face but the face of a stranger. I recoiled from it, even though she pitied me and tears rolled down her soft, rosy cheeks and the fragrance of her body was still a delight to my senses. But all round in the dark room there were bodies lying very still on their narrow cots, or tossing about and moaning in their sleep, or with fierce, pained eyes watching intently in the gloom. And the woman was a stranger. Then she suddenly stooped down and sobbed and kissed me on the forehead, and I hid my head under the clothes and became vague once more, unable to disclose my important communication.

Next I found myself before a doctor who had a cruel face. He spoke angrily to me. I felt that he was an enemy, so I rushed at him to strike him, but some people held me and doused the top of my head with a heavy shower of cold water. Then I was locked in a cell which was quite empty. There were iron bars on the window. I stayed there for a long time walking about. Now and again a man with a very brutal face looked into the cell and asked me some question which I could not understand. Each time the man entered I tried to tell him the very important thing that lay heavy on my mind. But he just laughed and went out again, locking the door after him. At last I fell down on the floor with exhaustion, and I next remembered finding myself in bed in a long room, beside a young man who smiled at me in a very friendly way and whispered an interminable story about a railway which he intended to build in Canada. I knew that the young man was mad, and that the other wild-eyed men in the room were all mad, but I could not understand why I was placed there among them.

Later I again saw the doctor whose face had appeared cruel to me and whom I tried to attack. His face no longer looked cruel and he spoke to me in a kindly fashion. I said I wished to speak to him privately, and I was brought into another room, where I told him what had happened to me and how worried I was because I could not find the transport officer whom I was guiding into the front line. He told me not to worry about the transport officer, that he had very likely found the front line on his own account and that I was going to England. Then I discovered that my voice had made no sound from the time the man struck me on the face with his blood-stained hand until the water had been poured on my head.

"But you were mad," said a voice, "just as mad as the smiling young Canadian who was building his interminable railway, or the Australian across the room who was hatching eggs in his right lung."

"Then have I been mad ever since?"

"Yes. You have been mad ever since. You were sent from one hospital to another and finally discharged from King George V hospital in Dublin for melancholia acuta. Your whole conduct since had been a proof of your insanity. And now you imagine that you are going to make a fortune betting on race-horses. Mad, mad. You never recovered from that bursting shell. The other two were luckier than you. You have to go through life with that shell bursting in your head."

I stood up, reduced to a state of coma by this savage thought. By then the place was crowded, and as I wandered about I was continually being jostled by people who were in a hurry to make their bets on the first race. I no longer felt decided about my bet on the race. Whereas one voice urged me not to change my plans but to go boldly to the guichet and wager one thousand francs on my selection, another querulous voice pointed out that I had enough money to support me for ten weeks in Brittany, during which time I could write enough to put me solidly on my feet. It would be criminal to deprive myself of this chance. And yet, I could see the horse in my imagination romping home unchallenged at a long price. It was very hot and perspiration poured from my face trying to arrive at a decision. And then I heard a Frenchman say to a friend: "*Moi, j'ai joué Why Worry Deux. Et toi? Qu'est-ce que tu as fait?*" I answered him in my mind by saying, "*Moi aussi,*" as I rushed off to bet, hauling a thousand franc note from my pocket as I ran. As soon as I got my ticket I wandered out on to the lawn in front of the stand, hardly able to breathe.

They had just finished rolling up the carpet that had been spread across the track from the pelouse to the public enclosure. The stands were crowded, and people were watching the groups of beautiful young women who marched up and down the green sward, parading their dresses. There was glorious sunlight. I thought joyously:

"Let me surrender completely to this splendid folly during the few minutes that remain before the winning horse passes the post. Win or lose, I can enjoy it no more afterwards."

Then I looked all round and tried to revel in the scene, but by some freak of the imagination I saw a rabbit that had lost its way one morning in a cliff at home. I was fishing a little after dawn on a low rock that jutted westwards far out into the sea. The cliff curved deeply westwards over my head and at the base of the curve there was a hollow. The cliff rose on either side of this hollow and there was a deep fissure in the middle of it. The prowling rabbit had entered this fissure where it began at the hollow. Apparently he was an adventurous fellow, for he followed it a long way, and being unable to find his road back, he kept trying to clamber upwards to the summit. Up and down he ran, his movements becoming more and more excited. Even at that distance I could hear his pitiful squealing. And then he halted on a ledge, evidently paralysed with fear. Two carrion crows appeared in the sky above him. I shouted in order to drive them away. My shout re-echoed among the concave cliffs and the rabbit was roused into activity by it. But alas, he leaped in terror, missed his footing and hurtled down into the sea. With a hoarse croak, the carrion birds swooped after him, but they rose again. A rolling wave engulfed the little carcass.

And instead of revelling in the gorgeous scene, I fell to moping on the horrible phenomenon of death; how it appears from out the belly of the radiant morning to still the beating of the merry heart that basks in the sun of love. Silken flanks that canter over the grass, with peacock-coated pigmies rigid in their saddles, and gaudy harlots on parade before a golden idol, out of whose jaws the lynx-eyed merchants rush babbling their bids. Ten million years and they were tiny bladders floating in a warm pool, whence they climbed the cliff unto the shape of monstrous elephants and whales and megalomaniac men begetting gods in their fantastic brains. Ten million years and all may pass once more into a savage wilderness of prowling stars. Or else the cliff will be surmounted.

"They're off." I stopped thinking and watched. I no longer cared what won, having convinced myself that the life of the individual was too momentary in relation to the life of the universe to allow one event more importance than another. Indeed! Only by standing as I was, without thought, watching with complete indifference a group of animals in movement, could a man live intelligently. And yet, as they approached, I began feverishly to search for the colours of the animal I had backed. Suddenly my heart stopped beating. A man had cried out: "*Why Worry Deux, tout seul.*" I closed my eyes, opened them again and saw three horses running neck to neck and then one horse pulled out in front of the others. It passed the post in front and I caught sight of the number on its side. It was my horse. I had won.

I waited until the number went up, in order to convince myself that I was not suffering from another hallucination. Then I went at once to the totalisator and stood by the window where I was to be paid out, lest that also might disappear. In due course, the dividend was announced and I received my money. I had won about five thousand francs.

"That's nothing," I said to myself. "I'll go through the card. I'm bound to win to-day, no matter what I back. Wasn't it lucky that I lost my typewriter? I'll win masses of money. By God! I don't think I'll go to Brittany at all. I'll stay on in Paris until the flat-racing season comes to a close and really feather my nest in proper fashion. Then I'll set my affairs in order, as they say, and set out towards the East with the first snow. I might bring Harold along. We could set out from the Pool of London, having chartered an old tramp steamer and a crew of topers. We'll use beer as ballast and put in at any port that takes our fancy. Conversation, chess, good drinking will carry us merrily as far as Bangkok.

Then we'll cruise around casually among those islands, wherever they are, at the foot of the Asiatic continent. Then slowly on to the Fijis and the Samoan islands. Drop into Sydney to see a cricket match, or prowl into New Zealand to see a game of rugger. Ho! What a merry life we'll lead. In any case, it's about time to clear out of Europe before the crash comes. Let the crazy wretches fight it out among themselves. By the time we come back, if ever, the world will be a better place."

Engrossed in this fantastic reverie I had not noticed myself heading for the bar, and indeed I had ordered a glass of champagne before I realized what I was doing. Hastily I put it aside and ordered a glass of lemonade instead. Now that I was a rich man and about to take up the career of a professional gambler, I must keep a stern hold over myself. I drank my lemonade and went out under the trees to dream of the islands in the southern seas. I saw myself lying on the grass under a tropical tree, with a group of Samoan girls dancing near by, while I meditated on my weasel. No. I would banish the weasel. That was the forbidden fruit, the final madness the ambition to write. In any case . . .

"Let's have a small bet on the second race," I said to myself, " just to prove my infallibility."

I strolled over to the hundred-franc booth and bought a ticket for a horse that I picked out at random. Then I went out and sat on the stand to continue my dream. It was magnificent. Perhaps, after all, it might be more interesting to live in London, surround myself with brilliant wits and start a newspaper to satirize society. I began to see how difficult it was being rich, what with the unlimited variety of my desires and the drawback of merely having five senses, one brain and a body that lacked the power to be ubiquitous.

My horse won easily, but I did not move from the stand, since I now felt that I was far beyond being concerned with such paltry sums. However, the few hundred francs I had won would come in handy for tips, so I went and collected them. Then I walked around with my dream. By now I was beginning to get tired of my riches and I remembered Bunin's story about *The Gentleman from San Francisco*. In my small way I was being quite as vulgar as the American millionaire, and I was certain to be far more unhappy than he, being more intelligent. To my disgust, I recollected that all the rich people whom I had ever met suffered from a peculiar disease, a state of mental boredom from which only the most idiotic activities seemed able to rouse them. A newspaper to satirize society! How ridiculous compared to the barrel of Diogenes and that Greek's request for clear access to the sunlight!

"If we are climbing a cliff, we of the human species, it is surely with our intellects that we are to reach the summit. We lack the strength of the elephant, the speed of the deer, the organizational capacity of the bee. But we are pre-eminent in our power to imagine a state of perfection, which we call God and which we are trying to reach. That is the only cliff worth climbing. And if there is no cliff other than a monstrous delusion, which we have deliberately invented in order to protect ourselves against the discovery that annihilation is inevitable, even so it is good to believe in the delusion. God is indeed the protector of the beautiful in spirit against the base and the vulgar. But what is God for me? Is He the idea of Diogenes, or of Christ, or of Lenin? Should I strive to reach Him by living in a barrel, or by preaching brotherly love, or by endeavouring to increase man's power over his material environment? Or should I strive to sing of God like Shakespeare? To sing of all gods by singing of life's tragedy?"

Suddenly I felt aflame with the mania of creative ecstasy and I saw the weasel on the fence. He bowed to me, descended from the fence and ran, smelling the earth, to a small stream which was almost dried up by the heat of summer. For a little while he stood on a warm, yellow stone and then he passed to the far bank, where a little rabbit was basking in the sun near its hole. The weasel stared at the rabbit and then began to run around it. "See," I cried, "the little fellow is too young to be hypnotized. He is taking no notice of the weasel. Or is he amused by the queer dance of death?" And then the little rabbit's mother appeared from a clump of bushes near by. She screamed and sat up on her hind legs and then she rushed at the weasel. Then all became confused, and although I tried hard to see further into the outcome of this dance of death, it was in vain. I only saw the weasel once more peering over the fence, as he had been at the beginning.

"Come, come," I said. "What does it matter? I'll go and back this horse. Five thousand years from now, even Shakespeare's name will be no longer a memory. Ho, vanity! Perhaps indeed his powerful rhyme will outlive the monuments of princes, but it cannot outlive death which clutches all things in its jaws, even the earth itself and the proud sun with all its fire."

I went over to bet on the third race. I was now feeling very tired; so tired that I did not trouble to decide how much I was going to invest. I hauled out from my pocket two hundred francs and passed them through the little window. Then I wandered about the paddock, being too bored to go and watch the race. Again my animal won. It did not interest me, until I saw the dividend announced and discovered that he returned about two hundred and twenty-five francs to ten. Then, indeed, I jumped to my feet in a rage.

"My God! Twenty to one. If I had bet my winnings on the first race, I'd have won a hundred thousand francs. Twelve hundred pounds. Never mind. All told I've won a hundred and fifteen pounds. I'll put it all on Goyescas."

Trembling with excitement I went to collect my money, and when I had received it, I ran across to bet. I wagered ten thousand francs, took the tickets and went out on to the stand. I climbed to the very top, sat down and counted what money I had left. I had a little over fifteen hundred francs. If I lost, I would arrive in Brittany with about a thousand francs. In a few weeks I would be penniless. Very likely I had lost the power to write. What would happen to me or to my wife and little daughter, who were depending on me? About myself I did not care much, but they . . .

I stood up and said to myself:

"Go to the clerk who took the money and explain the

position to him. He'll give it back to you. Perhaps he, too, is . . ."

I shrugged my shoulders and sat down again. Impossible! That money was already caught in the machine, swallowed up by it, just as the weasel sucked the blood from the rabbit, just as the carrion swooped, just as the whores paraded, all sucked and pecked and filched, all of us preying on one another and consummate horror, all to be destroyed in death, like a host of locusts, that by their devilish multiplication devour and lay waste whatever is green and beautiful and succulent.

"Shame! Shame! Have we not eyes that catch beauty in their fine-wrought mirrors and tuneful ears, wherein blessed harmony is recorded and that great lord, the human intellect, sitting on his judgment seat, to tell us what is good and evil? Why then do we live as blindly as the locusts? Why do I stake my destiny on a horse's thighs and panting lungs? Why are all ears deaf and all eyes blind and all tongues dumb to beauty and harmony and to the voices of the prophets?"

Lo! I saw the earth in flower, a great carpet of delicious blossoms. Then a malignant cloud descended from the sky and overspread the earth, blasting all its beauty, until it became a barren wilderness. And all the people who had lived within the gorgeous shelter of the flowers were now exposed and shivering in their nakedness. They began to delve into the earth, but the ground was rocky, and being unable to hide themselves they ran to and fro, screaming in despair: "Out of the darkness we cry out to thee, O Lord." But there was no Lord to hear them and soon they all fell down on the rocks and died.

Then there was dead silence. I could hear nothing, although the people about me were obviously talking in loud voices, pointing with their hands and stamping their feet. They were crying out in bitter darkness, or else scaling cliffs, or being swooped upon by carrion birds, or drinking from the necks of broken bottles in holes where shells were bursting into flame and red-hot fragments.

And then I said aloud:

"Of course it had to be."

I slowly walked down from the stand with the others, stunned and terrified. Maccaroni had won. Goyescas had never showed up for a moment with a winning chance. I had lost. I was lost. All was lost. A rabbit squealing.

## VI

I GOT back to my hotel, packed my bag, paid my bill and went to the Montparnasse station. I felt like a criminal fleeing from justice. A hunted man looking for a place to hide. I got a ticket for Quimper and went to the train. There was still three-quarters of an hour to wait. I bought a cubicle in the second-class sleeping carriage as I felt very exhausted after my experiences at the races and I was afraid I might get ill once more if I sat up all night in my clothes. At all costs I must get fit now and work. Having secured my berth, I went to the restaurant to get some food. That also was very necessary. In order to keep myself from thinking I went to the bookstall for something to read. I chose a life of Paul Verlaine that had just been published. Then I sat down in the restaurant and ordered dinner. While I was waiting to get served I opened the book and began to read.

After glancing at a few pages I put it away in anger. The author, whoever he was, wrote very badly and yet, in spite of his lack of talent, he adopted a superior attitude towards the poor, unhappy man whose life he was attempting to dissect for the bawdy mob.

" Bah! " I thought. " Can anything be more obscene than these literary grave-robbers? Tchekoff said that critics were like gad-flies worrying a labouring horse, but these men who write biographies of eminent writers nowadays are far more vicious. For them, the presence of syphilis in the blood of Guy de Maupassant is more important than that great writer's genius. They crow with glee when they discover that Dostoieffsky pawned his wife's wedding-ring in order to gamble, or that he crawled on his hands and knees up flights of stairs in order to touch the floor with his forehead at the feet of his mistress. I have read a life of Baudelaire in which the author discussed at great length the question of that poet's impotence and ended by coming to the conclusion that he had never been physically intimate with his coloured paramour. I once met a literary man, well known in London, who whispered to me with a snigger that Tolstoi had assaulted a peasant woman at the age of eighty. Even the obscurity which a kind fate cast over the life of Shakespeare has been pierced by wretches seeking proofs of his homosexuality. D. H. Lawrence was no sooner dead than the literary ghouls held up with maniacal delight the defects of his mortal nature, in order to cloud the shining glory of his intellect. How true it is that "censure is a tax levied by the public on men of eminence." The law of libel protects the living from the insults of the printed word, but rumour is a handy tool in the hands of spiteful slanderers, who take a malign pleasure in spitting on their superiors. Truly this is an age in which the race is to the mean, an age in which the scum of society sets the pace for aristocracy. An age in which greatness is denied its dignity and is compelled to go abroad in its nakedness. Or was it always so? "For slander's mark was ever yet the fair," said Shakespeare. Then why should I, a pigmy scribbler of crude words, take umbrage at offence, when that almighty lord of music deigned to have his sublime verses first sung to tavern sots? Let the unclean vermin feast on the corrupt flesh. They cannot touch the soul.

And yet tears welled behind my eyes and I cried out within myself for the compassion of my fellow-men. Not the compassion of the mean and selfish, but the compassion of the simple, sincere people, who judge not lest they might be judged, who realize that the just man falls seven times a day, who know that pity and love shine through the eyes and give warmth by their glance and need neither hands, nor feet, nor riches to bring solace to the sufferer. "Ní h-é lá na gaoithe lá na scolb." When the storm is in its fury is not the time to make fast the thatch.

I looked up into the face of the waitress who was laying food before me. Evidently she was struck by my distraught appearance, for she bent down and said gently:

"Are you ill?"

"No," I said, "but I lost my money at the races and I feel worried and lonely."

"Never mind," she said softly. "Money is not so important in life as the rich imagine. Cheer up, bright eyes."

She patted me gaily on the arm and went away, and then I felt comforted. Then I thought with shame how different had been my own conduct towards the American woman. But did the American woman deserve pity?

Suddenly I saw another woman in Hyde Park on a dark winter's evening. There was a bitter wind and yet she wore no overcoat, but just a tiny bit of shabby fur around her throat. I had come to listen to the people arguing at the Marble Arch, being in a very gloomy mood and not knowing where to seek refuge from my thoughts during the evening. I found myself face to face with this poor girl. She smiled at me, and I could see her wan, sickly face under the light of a lamp. There were red daubs of paint on her cheeks. Her teeth were broken and turned almost black by some disease. She was shivering. Her hip bones stood out against her shabby, blue skirt. Her smile was awful, like the grin on the face of a corpse whose jaw has fallen loose.

"Will you come for a walk?" she said.

I nodded without speaking. She took my arm and we walked away down the park under the trees, from which drops of rain left in the branches by a recent shower were being shaken by the fierce wind on to our heads. The girl shivered and clung close to my body for warmth, and she began to chatter.

"A night like this is awful for us girls," she said.

I started. I had hardly been aware of her presence, but now I looked at her with interest, for until then it had not struck me as possible that she could be a street girl. She was so ugly and shabby and in all ways wretched. How could she hope to arouse desire even in the most drunken and indifferent man? And I asked her did she often come to the Park.

"This is the second time I came here," she answered. "I had a job in a factory at twenty-five bob a week, but we had to work twelve hours a day and I'm not very strong, so I took ill and was in bed for two, three weeks. Then when I came back the job was gone, so I had to take to this. God! This is worse than workin' ten hours a day, I can tell ye. Let's sit down on this seat. Could ye spare a few bob?"

"Yes, of course," I said. "Just a moment."

I halted in the middle of the path, put my hand in my pocket and took out my wallet. I had about twenty pounds in it. For a moment I thought of giving her the lot, but I changed my mind and gave her a five pound note. She stared at it and then she said angrily:

"Why are ye makin' a fool o' me?"

"Why? Take it. Please take it."

"Rats," she said. "You're a funny fellow."

"Don't you think I mean it?"

"You may mean it all right, but it isn't genuine."

"All right," I said, "come to a shop and I'll get it changed into smaller notes for you."

Suddenly she grabbed the note and began to kiss my hands. I pulled away my hands and said:

"None of that."

She put her arms around my waist and whispered: "Oh! You're a kind man. Won't you give me one kiss? I feel terribly lonely."

"No," I shouted, pushing her from me.

Then I strode away hurriedly. I could hear her sob aloud, and I felt that I had acted in a beastly way to the woman.

"Money is not so important in life as the rich imagine. Cheer up, bright eyes."

The waitress came back again and said that she had been having a discussion with the girl at the cash desk as to my nationality. I entered into a merry conversation with both of them, and presently, in the extraordinary way that contact with sympathetic people drives out all thought of worry, "takes one out of oneself," I was in high spirits. I went off to the train feeling certain that I had done well in coming to France and that I would succeed in regenerating myself.

The travellers were now going aboard, and there were a number of children going with their parents to Brittany for their summer holidays. It was a merry scene, but it made me long for my own child, and I hurried into my carriage lest the sight of these little heads sticking out of the windows might be too much for me. My carriage was empty, except for a plump woman of about thirty-five, who kept walking up and down the corridor restlessly. She looked at me very fiercely and marched up to the far end, where she leaned out of a window, puffing at a cigarette. I could not resist looking once more at the children, whose cries of joy were like arrows in my ears; holy arrows whose wounds gave the torture of love. And when I looked I saw a chubby little girl of about five being held out through a window, so that she could kiss her father good-bye. He was a funny little man, with a red face and a tub of a stomach, but the child was very beautiful. She had short golden curls and lovely round arms, which she twined around her father's neck. She kissed him and then put her little hands through his hair, crying out: "Come to see us soon, papa." Then she was drawn back into the carriage and the little father put his thumbs under the lapels of his coat and wagged his fingers, as proud as could be.

I envied the little red-faced man with the round stomach, and even when I saw his gaunt-faced wife thrust her head out of the window and hurl a torrent of language at him in the manner of a shrew, I still envied him. The good-natured little fellow shrugged his shoulders and fluttered his hands from the wrists and smiled at the lean hag who was the mother of his child.

"They have some point of contact with society," I thought. "They are not alone like me. I am a wanderer on the face of the earth. And let me not suppose I could ever be otherwise. So let me face this knowledge and make provision accordingly."

I returned to my cubicle and sat down on the bed again.

"Why must I remain a wanderer? When I get

older and more temperate in my passions I'll settle down and have a position in my local society, just like this little man with the fat stomach."

But I shook my head and said aloud:

"That is untrue. At this moment you long for the companionship of your wife and child, because you lost money at the races and you are afraid of the future. If you had won you wouldn't feel their need."

A mist came before my eyes. My head throbbed. My right knee began to quiver. I realized that the man with whom I had argued on the race-course had returned. There he was, beside me on the bed, smiling in a superior fashion. In a peculiar way he had changed places with me. On our previous meeting it was I who had come to torment him. Now it was he who had come to torment me.

"You are a fine sort of fellow," he said, " to take to Brittany with me. The first little bourgeois you see, packing off his wife and children to the seaside, you want to change places with him. Now let me tell you the truth about that little man. The joy on his face which you envied, when his little girl's arms were about his neck, was just simply his delight at getting rid of his wretched nag of a wife for a week or two. As soon as this train leaves he'll rush off to celebrate his freedom with his cronies. He'll get drunk, and if he has any money left afterwards, he'll buy the services of some pretty girl for the night. That's the sort of fellow he is. They are all like that, the paltry hypocrites."

"Indeed!" I retorted. "And who are you to sit in judgment on these hypocrites, as you call them? The only time I was really happy was when I was married. You may mock at tenderness and sentimental love, but let me tell you that a man who thinks himself above such things is a barren wretch, a monster without a soul."

"Rot," he cried. "You are a fool. Without me you would not have been happy at any time, because you would not have had the capacity for being really unhappy."

"I heard that before. That's what you said to the American woman."

"Shut up," he cried. "I'm going to silence you once and for all by telling you the truth. From beginning to end you had nothing to do with it, so if you feel any remorse of conscience, let that trouble you no more. I am your master and I'm going to remain your master to the end. An old man of the sea on your back. I am your pilot fish and I find your prey for you. Listen. What would you be without me? Just a common fellow of no particular distinction. As you are poor and without influence or rank, you would attract no attention whatsoever. You'd have to work like a slave in order to earn your living, and if you married you'd probably get a lean, ugly woman like the little fellow's wife. Being a nervous and timid man, you'd be at her mercy and she'd probably beat you, together with making you a cuckold with the milkman or the baker. You are very lucky to be my mask."

I shuddered and felt so terribly afraid of the man that I could make no answer, although I knew if I remained silent I must go on suffering his mastery for years to come and perhaps to the very end of my life; being hurled from pillar to post by his insane folly.

"This is how it happened," he continued. "I fell in love with her because she admired my work and because I found in her qualities that you lacked: sober judgment, a cultured mind, strength of character. She fell in love with me for a similar reason, in order to attach herself to my power of expression."

"Why must you dissect what is holy, the holiest thing in life, as if it were the entrails of a rat in the hands of a scientist? Why not be grateful for having received what is given to few people, a pure, unquestioning love that triumphed over the opposition of society as well as over penury, sickness and the outlawry of the Philistines?"

He remained silent for a little while, and I thought that I had defeated him. I was about to press home my victory when I became aware of his glittering eyes staring at me. I drew back in terror.

"Can it be possible that you don't know me yet?" he whispered. "Why! I'd cut off your hands and feet in order to write a phrase. I'd have you annihilated for the sake of creating something really perfect. What you call the holiest thing in life is holy when it is the food of the imagination. When it ceases to feed the imagination it ceases to be holy. It ceases to exist and the wise man deserts the empty store-room with the same speed that he would flee from a charnel-house that was full of pestilential smells. He seeks elsewhere. I took all she had to give and then I left her."

"But she is still with you."

"Of course, just as I am with her. Or just as we are both with our child. Love as distinct from passion is just getting used to people one likes. Once that is done, the people to whom one has got used and whom one likes always remain with one. But it's not necessary to be physically intimate with them or even to see them. As a matter of fact, when one gets used to a person one likes, it is repugnant to have physical intimacy with that person; certainly for a sensitive individual it is impossible, and we are not concerned with those who are not sensitive. You and I are very much so, are we not?"

"You are making fun of me," I whispered, "but even though I am but your mask, I am that portion of you that is seen by the world. You may despise me but you have a duty towards me."

"What is it, may I ask? How can a man have a duty towards the house he inhabits?"

"He should keep it clean. Only by doing so can he be comfortable in it. It is all very well for you to have your fine dreams and to consider yourself superior to the ordinary code of morality, but if I lose my self-respect through your disorderly conduct, the source of your inspiration will run dry. Nobody can do good work if he has lost his self-respect."

"On the contrary," he said, "it is only by living in a disorderly manner that a writer nowadays can maintain his self-respect. Otherwise he is sure to lose his inspiration by getting tamed into social respectability. To have money in the bank is more hurtful to a creative artist than the lewdest vice. The applause of the herd is equally dangerous, for it atrophies the imagination, instilling fear of losing by daring what he has already gained and found pleasing. You see, a creative artist is half man and half woman. The woman in him is always craving for luxury and public esteem, holding up her child for admiration, longing for the position of honour at a public banquet. But the man in him, the possessor of the seed, becomes corrupt and impotent under the influence of wealth and flattery. And for that reason he must always hold the woman on the flat of her back. He must take care to have himself considered a rogue and a vagabond, a bawdy roysterer, an enemy of society. He must be an angel of discontent. In that way he holds off the worship of the herd and is allowed to work in peace. He must be content to leave public applause and the luxuries begotten of it to such ephemeral creatures as actors, champion pugilists, jockeys, triumphant generals, the successful thieves of the stock exchange and all such individuals that have their paltry hour of glory. He must be as ruthless with himself as an ancient hermit scourging himself with a spiked thong. That way alone is the way to perfection for the creative writer."

"But nearly all great writers have been respectable citizens."

"Have they, indeed? Could anybody call Rabelais respectable? François Villon was equally disreputable. Baudelaire, Maupassant and even the self-righteous Rousseau would be asked to resign from any reputable London club. Even the crabbed little Voltaire managed to procure himself an opportunity of living in sin. Shakespeare deserted his wife and children by all accounts.

There is even a legend that he was put in jail for poaching. Marlow was killed in a drunken brawl. Defoe, whom I consider the greatest English novelist, knew far too much about pickpockets to warrant any plausibility for the belief that he was respectable. Goethe had more wives than a modern film actor. I defy you to show me a great writer who was not either a toper, or a profligate lecher at one time or other of his life. It has been truly said that the greater a man is, the greater is his potentiality for good and evil."

"That may be so," I said, "but the great man disciplines himself."

"Admittedly, but the severest form of discipline for the creative writer is to live dangerously, as Nietzsche said, or to accept Blake's contention that the only sin is desire repressed. If you show me the abstemious Titiano, sitting coldly at the head of his table, making sketches of the brilliant Venetian harlots with whom Aretino was having lewd pranks, I merely point out that the painter was following his natural inclination and that it was not for him a question of discipline or self-denial. Self-denial for me means a continual war on self-deceit, against intellectual cowardice, against everything that threatens to disturb the lordship of my mind over my environment. In order to carry on this war I must live alone, within the fortress of your body. Woe to anybody who tries to enter that fortress in order to share it with me."

"What a life!" I cried in despair. "Must this go on for ever?"

The man laughed gaily and whispered:

"It must go on till I have sucked the marrow from

your bones and drained the last drop of your blood; until you are a carcass stiff in death; until you feel no more the insurrection of your loins in answer to the fire of lust; until your eyes become indifferent to the sun; until your ears cease to strain for that wild call of life, which stands trembling in the distance, a virgin gorgeous in her beauty offering the flower of her maidenhood, a garden all in bloom and pollen carried on the gentle wind from perfumed cup to cup. Rise up and go again to look into the faces of those children and see them with my eyes, triumphant in the knowledge that my love has looked upon the face of God and therefore must eschew all human bondage."

The train began to move. I went out into the corridor. A group of children were singing in a carriage. Their lovely voices thrilled me and I felt purified. I saw the earth washed clean by an April shower and the sunbeams gleaming on the moist grass and smelt the fragrance of the sap from the budding trees. Ho! I saw the merry skylarks dotted on the air and the swift passage of the homing dove.

"All is holy," said the train. "Blessed are they who have sinned, for they alone can feel the joy of forgiveness."

### VII

HERE it is necessary for me to state, since I am attempting to tell the exact truth, whatever that is, about a particular phase of my life, that my journey into Brittany was my fourth attempt since last February to escape from my dilemma.

My first journey brought me to Spain, a country which has always been popular among Irishmen as a refuge in time of difficulty. On the first of March I crossed the Spanish frontier at Irun, bound for Seville, where I intended to live for six months, or until I had finished writing a novel that I had on hands. I reached Seville safely enough in spirit and found lodgings at a small hotel in the Calle O'Donnell, but I had not been more than an hour in the place when I knew that I had made a mistake. There is far less noise in New York than in Seville and the streets are far wider. I heartily cursed the romantic people who had told me about the peaceful grandeur of this ancient town, whereas I found a network of narrow, stinking lanes, crowded with clanking tramcars, whose passage forced one into smelly doorways, there not being enough room on the pavement. By day these noisy tramcars passed by my window, making it impossible to work. By night, gangs of rowdies discussed current politics in the street, making a din quite as hideous as that of the tramcars. Work? Impossible in Seville, where life solely consists of a long and noisy conversation.

After the first day, I abandoned all idea of settling in the town, so I sat in the lounge and tried to decide where I should go next. I met a young American girl in the lounge and I confided in her. She loved Spain and had attended the university of Madrid for some years. Now she was going on a tour of the country with her invalid mother.

" What is Cadiz like? " I said to her. " Now there

is a fine name for a town. It has always reminded me of a roan mare that I considered the most romantic thing in my neighbourhood when I was a little boy. A sort of golden romance."

She shrugged her shoulders and said:

"If you don't like Seville you won't like Cadiz. The smell there is worse. The smell there is really frightful."

"Ha!" I said. "I am possibly right in my belief that Spain is like a rugger team of old internationals. It looks well on paper but that's all. I feel certain that the only decent town in it is the town of Barcelona, which has nothing of the fandango about it."

"Oh, but you must see it before you judge it," she said. "It's not fair to sit here in this room and grouse about it without taking the trouble to look. That's so English."

"Indeed!" I said. "At this distance from London, I'm not so sure that the English are not the most reasonable excuse for the existence of the human race."

"You are being horrid," she said. "I was going to show you around Seville, but now I shan't."

"Please don't get offended," I cried anxiously, afraid that she was going to leave me. "I'm in a bad way. That's why I am making stupid remarks about this marvellous country, the birthplace of Cortez, Cervantes, bull-fighting, Argentina the dancer and the midday siesta. I am neurotic and that is why I appear to be a fool. I once met a fellow in Moscow, wearing a beard and a Russian blouse and looking exactly like a Russian from a short story by Tchekoff. You know, the very refined type of Russian who asks himself twenty times a day whether it's going to be strychnine or a plain revolver. This chap on acquaintance proved to be an Englishman and more rabidly anti-Russian than an exiled Russian prince. I asked him why he stayed in Moscow if he hated it so much. He explained to me that he stayed there for the reason that he felt normal in it. In common with everybody whom he knew he wanted to be elsewhere. Whereas in London, Paris, Vienna, Budapest, Rome or Madrid, he might know people who really liked to stay where they were. The curse of the neurotic person is that he always wants to be somewhere else. He is a nuisance to himself and to his friends. Please forgive me and show me Seville."

She did show me Seville. I stood in the majestic cathedral with her and saw the tomb of Christopher Columbus and listened to her expiate on how the symmetry of the building made her believe in God. Then we saw the Alcazar gardens and the great bath which Pedro made for his mistress. Then there was little else to see and I admitted to her that I would rather see a lot of selling platers run a five furlong race at Alexandra Park or listen to a pair of dockers having an argument in Walsh's bar on the North Wall. She said I was a barbarian.

"That may be," I said, "but I want a life that is harmonious, and here there is only death. Here are the remains of a former grandeur. This town has been dead for centuries. I want life. Where can I get it in Spain?"

"Very well, then," she said. "Go to Madrid. You'll get life there."

That evening a Swede tried to commit suicide at our

hotel. He had, apparently, arrived on the previous day with an American woman, on whom he was living. She left him and went to Barcelona. Then he put a revolver to a safe part of his chest, rang the bell and fired. When they got to his room, they found him suffering from a wound that was not very serious. He asked them to wire for his American friend. She took an aeroplane and flew back. She arrived in a state of great agitation and disturbed the whole hotel. I felt that I had had enough of Seville, so I boarded the train for Madrid that evening.

The American girl accompanied me to the train and said on bidding me good-bye:

"You really need somebody to look after you. Were it not for my invalid mother, I would get a mule and then we'd wander into the country until we found a nice fonda somewhere. You'd love it. I'd look after you and you'd write your novel."

"My dear girl," I said, "you are most kind and I hope that some time or other you'll find that fonda for yourself and the man who loves you, either in Spain or the stuffy interior of a New York skyscraper. Personally I have to find it alone."

"You'll hardly find it in Madrid," she said.

"I'll find Goya there," I said.

In the morning I reached Madrid and took a room in a pension on the Prado. The young fellow who carried my bag from the station near by suggested that I should accompany him to the bull-fight that afternoon. I agreed and gave him the money to buy the tickets. At two o'clock he came to fetch me. I noticed that he scrutinized my dress with great care.

"Excuse me," he said, "but have you got a white handkerchief?"

"Why?"

"It's impossible to go to a bull-fight without a white handkerchief. At least I presume you want to do it properly."

"Why not?" I said. "I'll get one if it's *de rigueur*."

After all, as I discovered later, as a form of idiocy it was more intelligible than having to wear a top-hat among the best people at Ascot or a black suit to eat dinner. When my white handkerchief was properly fixed in the outside breast-pocket of my coat, the little fellow and myself set forth. He was about the size of an apprentice jockey and he looked all over a pickpocket, a quick-moving, fast-speaking guttersnipe, a type that is produced by all the great cities of the world, exactly similar in habits, speech, deportment and size, from Tokio to London.

Having gone through a park, which he told me was a useful place at night for those who preferred the simple pleasures of the poor to paying exorbitant prices for temporary accommodation in an hotel, we got on a tube train and arrived in the neighbourhood of the bull-ring. Here my guide got very excited and changed from French to Spanish in order to curse with greater eloquence.

"What's the matter, mate?" I said.

"The cigars!" he cried. "Good Lord Almighty! You don't imagine we can show our faces in the ring without having cigars in our mouths?"

"Let's get some, then," I said.

However, it was difficult to do so near the bull-ring,

since hundreds of Spaniards had forgotten their cigars and had bought up the supplies of cigars in the local shops before our arrival. My guide gave some money to two young boys, who said they knew an unlicensed shop near by. We waited for them to return for ten minutes and then my guide began to get nervous once more. Had they done a bunk? I assured him that it was more than likely.

"No," he said coldly. "If it were your money they would not come back, because you are a foreigner. But I am a Madrileno, so they'll come back with my money."

Presently the boys returned at a run with the cigars. The little guide's face brightened. We lit cigars and went into the ring and sat on a bench among rows upon rows of people who had white handkerchiefs and cigars.

It was the first time I had been in a bull-ring and I confess that I was very disappointed with it at first sight. Indeed, I had vaguely come that afternoon with the idea of becoming an addict of this new bull-worship, which has become the religion of so many writers nowadays. Since one must worship something in order to spur one to creative activity, why not the bull? In other words, I thought that an enthusiasm for bull-fighting might be a means of escape from my world-weariness. I had read Hemingway, D. H. Lawrence, Blasco Ibañez and others on that ancient pastime, together with interesting myself in the various controversies that appear now and again in the newspapers about the cruelty of goring horses in bull-rings. So that I felt that a bull-fight was a magnificent spectacle at least. But the ring looked so much like Blackfriars ring on a Sunday afternoon that I was horribly disappointed. And I thought how much nicer it would be on a race-course, or looking at the pictures in the museum on the Prado, or lying on the grass in the park with a pretty girl.

However, I began to share the excitement of the crowd as the moment approached for the commencement of the performance. My guide was almost in hysterics. With tears in his eyes, he told me how he had often, as a little boy, stolen money from his mother in order to attend a bull-fight.

"That's splendid," I said.

"Yes," he said. "It proves that I had the makings in me of a real bull-fight fan."

"Good Lord! Yes," I said. "It was a splendid beginning."

"Watch," he cried, pointing to the clock. "I bet you a peseta that the show'll start exactly to the second. It's wonderful how it starts on time."

It did, and the crowd gave the fact that it started on time a special cheer. I watched eagerly as the parade of the showmen deployed into the ring.

"It's the greatest spectacle left in the world," cried my guide.

"How much better they do it in Hollywood!" I thought. "These fellows don't march in step and none of them are as attractive to look at as Valentino, who acted in 'Blood and Sand.'"

The president threw down the key, the performers got into position and the bull was let loose in the ring. He chased everybody he saw and they all fled from him, only to sneak out again and make passes at him with their capes. Then a picador came out on his horse. He did not get far, as the wretched animal sank down in the middle, spreading wide its legs. A few men got under it and lifted it up. I laughed outright at the ludicrousness of anybody stealing from his mother in order to see a miserable animal like that on exhibition. By lashing and pushing and lifting the horse, they got it around the ring to where the bull could see it. The bull was not very brave, or else he liked horses, for he refused to attack the blindfolded old crock, whose sides were covered with something like a mattress. At last, however, he got sufficiently irritated by the abuse of the picador. He rushed at the picador and gored the horse's side. The picador thrust the point of his lance into the bull's back. The bull crushed the horse against the railing of the arena and the picador at once threw himself over the rails, abandoning his mount to the bull, who drew back and gored the wretched horse once more. This time his horns got well under the mattress. He lifted the poor old carcass up by the front and then shook his head. Then he drew back once more, attracted by the cries of the cape men, who came worrying him. He pursued the capes and the horse stood still against the fence, just like a man dead drunk, with a great stream of blood falling from its belly. A man came up to it quickly behind the rails, plunged a dagger into its head and the animal dropped down on to its gore.

Nobody seemed to notice the death of the horse except myself and a Frenchwoman who sat on my right. She said the whole thing was too brutal for her to endure and demanded to be taken away by her husband. Her husband, however, was obviously an afficionado of the game, for he answered her angrily and then continued to wave his handkerchief.

"Pay attention," said my guide, digging me in the ribs. "Wave your handkerchief and shout. Morales is magnificent to-day."

Suddenly I forgot about the horror inspired in me by the blood pouring from the horse's bowels and I became intoxicated by the general excitement. The banderillero had already placed his darts in the bull and that animal was now being prepared for its death by the matador, an individual called Morales, who seemed popular among the crowd. Now the bull and the man were alone in the ring and I began to understand the fascination of this extraordinary sport. I found myself shouting, "*Olle, olle*" and "*Muy Valiente*" and "*Que gracia*," as excitedly as the guide, at each beautiful pass which Morales made with the muleta. I waved my white handkerchief and the stump of my cigar, and I swore that I would live for ever in Spain during the summer and cross to Mexico for the winter, in order to witness this marvellous dance of death all the year round.

Morales, however, made a sorry attempt at killing the bull, which had finally to be stabbed behind the ear, amid the howls of the mob. I thought they were cursing the fighter and asked the guide had the man deteriorated or what was the matter.

"It's the bull," he said, looking at me in scorn. "That coward of a bull we are cursing. It was not the fault of Morales."

The carcass was quickly hauled out of the arena by

fast galloping mules, the sand was straightened out and another animal entered the ring. This was a dull fight, but in the third we were treated to a magnificent example of the bull-fighter's art by a young debutant, of whose name I only remember the word Gomez. The guide wept on my shoulder after Gomez had dispatched his bull in fine style at the first thrust of the sword.

"You have brought me luck," he said. "You are a lucky man, a very lucky man. You might have waited for years to see such an exhibition. You have witnessed the rise to fame of a man who is perhaps as great as El Gallo or Belmonte."

We lit fresh cigars in honour of the young fellow who was having a triumphal march around the arena, and when the last bull had been floored, the guide and myself climbed down into the sand, to get among the crowd who were gathered around the new popular hero. The bull was not yet quite dead and small boys were rushing up to him, kicking his sides and dabbing their hands in his blood with cries of joy. The young bull-fighter was daubed in the face with blood from the bull's ear, exactly as if he were a young English woman of good family attending her first kill at a fox hunt.

Then I left my guide and returned to my pension. That night I was disturbed in my sleep with dreams about bull-fighting and by the following morning I had come to the conclusion that the worship of the bull was not sufficient incentive to keeping me at work in Spain. A conversation which I had at lunch with a fine old Frenchman convinced me that I was right.

"The vice of sadism," he said calmly, "is regrettable

in princes and men of eminence, who are sufficiently delicate to indulge their passion for it in secret. When it is practised in public by the mass of common people it is an abomination which I cannot persuade myself to witness. But mark you, I do not condemn Spain or the Spanish character on this account. I have seen near Valencia their mode of cultivating oranges, which persuades me that the Spaniards are magnificent farmers. Proficiency in the art of agriculture in any respect, even in the production of a solitary fruit, atones for many a vice. As I said before, only brilliant and useful people can afford to have vices."

After that, I spent two days in the museum looking at the pictures, in an attempt to fasten myself on Madrid and set to work; but though I stood in rapture for hours without moving before the masterpieces of Goya, the rapture was purely receptive and feminine. It did not generate a desire to create anything on my own account. Then I thought it might be a good thing to meet some of the Madrid intellectuals and become interested in the life of the country, as a result of contact with their creative enthusiasm, should I find them to possess any.

I thought that the best way to become acquainted with the intellectuals would be through my publishers, so I tracked them down after some difficulty on the outskirts of the city. The man whom I interviewed was a German, of an intellectual elasticity and graciousness of manner typical of that subtle race. I tried to make known my identity in broken Spanish. He stared at me like a dazed bull.

" *Ye barle franthez,*" he roared.

I then tried to explain myself in French, but he soon shouted at me in English:

"That language forgot have. What?"

Whereupon I burst out laughing and the German joined me, with obvious pleasure. Then, tapping his chest and my own, I said slowly:

"You, my books, published, have."

"Ha!" he cried, and again the dazed look came into his eyes. "What means that? Published? Such a thing. Why?"

"Hurrah!" I cried in despair, waving my hand above my head.

"Hurrah!" said the German. "*Ver gut.*"

"That's all right," I said, getting to my feet. "Service. So sorry. *Go d-tachtaigh an diabhal thu.*"

"Hurrah!" said the German once more, smiling affectionately.

"Go to blazes," I said, rushing out of his office.

I returned to my room, packed my bag and took the train to Toledo, hoping to achieve my purpose by looking at the paintings of El Greco. After a night's rest I proceeded to examine this town. First of all, I stood on the highest point in the town and looked down into the broad, flat land that surrounds it. I was strangely moved by the prospect, and for the first time since I had come to Spain my eyes were opened to the majesty of that great country. My blood ran hot and I swore in exaltation that here at last I had found a place to work, in this watch-tower above the yellow plains. Then I hurried down from the height and left the town, in order to enter it once more with new eyes.

Over the gate I read: "Blasphemy and begging are forbidden in this city." Then I passed under the ancient arch and was immediately besieged by a gang of beggars, who blasphemed most frightfully on being refused. I reached the principal square, where I was surrounded by guides, who implored me in several languages to purchase their services. I chose a young fellow who said nothing at all, but kept winking at me politely and made gestures with his hands and lips, to explain in a very forcible way that the others were thieves and swindlers. The young man and I struck a bargain. Then we set forth to view the town. After having gently dissuaded him from forcing me into fifteen different shops, where tourists are persuaded to buy articles representative of the craftsmanship of Toledo steel workers, he at last agreed to show me what I wanted. I saw a great number of El Greco's works, but whether it was the chatter of the guide or a lack of sympathy with the painter's genius, I was in no way moved.

After lunch we attacked the cathedral. The guide drew my attention to a change in the name of the street that runs between the entrance to the cathedral and the archbishop's palace.

"Since the revolution it has become Calle Carlos Marx," he said with obvious glee.

"That's a poor joke," I said. "Marxism is something more important than a paint-brush in the hands of a nocturnal nasty-boy. This museum of Christian grandeur, this town of Toledo should be left intact, with its beggars, its hordes of priests, its poxy harlots and its magnificent spoils of conquest and discovery in gold, silver, bronze, tapestries, masterpieces of architecture and painting and craftsmanship. The name of Marx is not, after all, a name that should be written on all walls wherever there are walls, but only on the walls of banks and stock exchanges, on dynamos, steam-engines and skyscrapers, on air-ships and air-tight metal spheres catapulted into the airless wastes where lodge the unknown planets, on which future man shall build cathedrals and chant High Masses to unborn Christs. Come. Let us see the cathedral."

What a gruesome atmosphere! It smelt of death and starvation, even though it was crowded with priests and worshippers and within its walls there was sufficient wealth to buy a city of considerable size. What a contrast to the poverty of the citizens was presented by the magnificence of its treasures! I was glad to leave it, for it made me angry, almost into agreeing with the men who had written the name of Carlos Marx on its rump.

"I've seen enough of death," I told the guide. "Let us go to a tavern and drink ourselves back to life with a pig of wine."

"We'll go to Pedro's," he said.

Thither we went and presently we were emptying the pigskin in good company. When we had laid such a good stock within our own skins as made us merry, we went into the cellar and filled our goblets from the snouts of several pigs, until some of the company, being of a squeamish appetite, fell down on the floor. The rest of us then adjourned to an eating-house, where we ate lavishly of snails done in the Spanish way. Then we came back to Pedro's and drank some more.

"Now," said my guide, "we shall continue our examination of this city, for the most interesting part of it can only be seen by night."

The brothels to which he brought us smelt of death as much as the cathedral had done. In one place there were a pair of musicians who were blind and in another place the proprietress was paralysed.

"Let us eat more snails," I said.

In the morning I was violently ill from a surfeit of snails, and as soon as I was able to move, I made the best of my way back to London. After a short rest I again took to the road, now convinced that Connemara would be my salvation. On the train from Galway to Clifton I met an Englishman, who was going to that town for a fortnight in search of an improvement in his health. I thought this very odd, for nobody but a fool could expect the Connemara climate to be health-giving at that time of year. The local police also thought it odd and immediately came to the conclusion that the pair of us were journalistic spies, inquiring into a recent scandal. The Englishman and myself spent twenty-four hours persuading the police and the principal inhabitants that we were honest travellers, but that entailed the consumption of so much Guinness's stout that snails and the pigskin at Toleda seemed to me far more likely to excite the imagination into productive activity than rain, porter and public suspicion at Clifton. So I took a wild leap and landed at Dieppe in Normandy without drawing breath.

"Ha!" I cried. "Here I am on the sacred soil of France. Now I can work."

In order to celebrate my arrival in the land of liberty,

I drank a quantity of cider with a sailor, who proved to be a professional thief. Then I struck up with an accordion player, who amused me for some time with his tunes and then brought me to a cabaret, for which he was a tout. I drank in the cabaret until the small hours of the morning and then set out for my hotel. On the way I was accosted by two sailors, who asked me for money. I searched my pockets and found nothing. On my explaining to them that my pockets were empty, one of them struck me on the side of the head with a stone and then they both ran away. The wound began to bleed profusely and I wandered about, stunned, until I saw a light shining through an open door. I entered this house and asked for help, but the inhabitants, being startled by my distraught manner and my bloody face, instead of giving me help sent for the police. The policeman promptly dragged me to the police station and threw me into a cell.

I regained consciousness some hours later to find myself in pitch darkness, except for a glimmer of dull light that came through a tiny, barred peep-hole. The wound in my head pained exceedingly. I put up my hand and found that my hair was clotted with blood, over the spot where I had been hit.

"My God!" I cried. "At last it has happened. Now I am done for."

Ever since that dreadful night at Langemarck I had been afraid of a blow on the head. I recalled what the doctor had said at the medical board which discharged me from the army: "Avoid hot climates, over-excitement of any kind, and especially games like boxing or rugby football, where your head might get injured." Now it had happened.

In a frenzy I tried to recall how it had happened; how I had got into this strange place, where there was no light except a dull glimmer through a tiny, barred peep-hole; where there was a stench of excrement; where I was lying on a board. But I could only remember leaving the cabaret and walking along the cobbled dock-side. After that, recollection became a humming noise of shouting, curses and terror, For a short while, panic almost gained the mastery, suggesting that I had committed some heinous crime, for which I would be condemned to death. I lay still, holding my breath, in an effort to master this panic. My imagination was tremendously active, and in a few seconds it had rehearsed the whole process of my trial, conviction and execution. About my crime it remained vague in order to heighten the terror caused by it. And then I suddenly attained mastery over this panic. I smiled in the darkness and reflected with great joy that I had at last experienced a repetition of that emotion of profound fear which I had experienced once before, on the day they threw water over my head, stripped me and locked me in an empty cell at Etaples. Dostoieffsky in a white shirt waiting for the soldiers to fire. In these moments of supreme fear all life stands naked. Every fibre of the being is on tip-toe struggling to achieve omniscience before life becomes extinct. And from this struggle the imagination comes forth triumphant, having drained the energy of the various appetites that in normal life do check its flight.

I began to act the caged criminal, having granted him

the widest range conceivable for his malefactions, from a common murderer to a maniacal anti-Christ who had planned the destruction of his species. I felt the evil joy of the super-criminal in being alone against humanity. I rose from the stinking boards and felt my way charily in the darkness towards the glimmer of light that came through the peep-hole. Suddenly I fell into what I thought was a pit; but it was only a drop of about eighteen inches from the wooden couch, which filled all the rear of the cell, to a narrow trench between the couch and the door. I got to my feet and tried to look through the peep-hole, but the slide was drawn over it and I could see nothing. Then I felt all over the door and discovered how massive it was. It was impossible to escape. My spirits sank and I assumed the terrible despair of the condemned man who is waiting for his executioner to appear. I sat on the edge of the couch, dropped my arms between my knees and began to think. But to my surprise I could not think, and then I realized with bitterness that a doomed or even jailed man, if in darkness, cannot think, since there is nothing to excite the mind. I sat in nothingness.

Slowly another form of panic overpowered me, so that I jumped to my feet and hurled myself at the door, on which I banged with my fists. I shouted, asking to be released. I was no longer a criminal, but a just person against whom an outrage had been committed. After some time the slide was withdrawn from the peep-hole and a cruel face stared at me. I asked to be allowed to the lavatory. He shrugged his shoulders and said there was plenty of room in the cell. Then he grinned and closed the slide. I shouted at him to bring me at least a glass of water, but he only answered with a laugh, and then I heard his footsteps moving away.

Many hours later they took me from the cell and brought me upstairs to an official who read out to me a long list of my offences, which included breaking into a house, threatening the inhabitants and doing damage to the furniture. I explained to the official, as well as I could, for I was still vague about the affair, what had happened, but he smiled in a knowing way and insisted on maintaining that I was a foreign criminal, a Scandinavian of some sort, who had entered Dieppe in order to start a reign of terror.

"Are you a German by any chance?" he said.

"No," I answered.

"You might as well confess," he said, "before we confront you with the honest citizens whom you have assaulted."

"I have nothing to confess," I cried, "except that I have been wounded and then imprisoned when I asked for help. Do you call that French justice?"

"I warn you," he said, "that it will go badly with you if you are offensive to France."

"Oh, yes," said the policeman who had brought me from the cell. "He kept shouting that France was a dirty country."

"Oh! He has said that, has he?" cried the official. "We'll show him."

"Without wishing to be offensive to France," I said, "I do maintain that it is contrary to civilized usage to force prisoners to foul their cells."

"Silence," they both cried.

My accusers were then brought into the room, a man with his wife and daughter.

"That is the man," they said in answer to the official's question.

However, on his inquiring what I had done, they had to admit, much to the official's disgust, that I had merely asked for a towel and water to wash my wound, that they had been terrified and run into an inner room, and that I had then spoken loudly in a foreign language which they understood to be German. They said they had no wish to proceed with the case, provided I repaired the damage done.

"What damage did I do?" I cried.

"You upset a dish of water," said the woman, "and pushed the furniture about. A photograph of my uncle was thrown to the floor, but the chief damage was to our nerves. We shall all probably have to consult a doctor, and that is expensive, as everybody knows."

"I'll pay whatever you want," I cried.

"Don't shout at respectable citizens," cried the officials. "It is obvious that you are not in the habit of consorting with respectable people. Take him back to his cell."

I was taken back to the cell, where I remained for some time, until I was again released and brought into the day-room. There I met an Englishman whom one of the police had fetched. He very kindly agreed to send a telegram to London for me and to notify the consul of my predicament. Then I was sent back into the cell to sleep, in the company of a homeless man who was being given a shelter for the night. The man had already lain down, taken off his boots and covered himself with the filthy blankets when I entered. I found the smell of the blankets and the propinquity of the unknown man so repulsive that I could not lie down, even though I was on the point of collapse from exhaustion. So I sat on the edge of the couch.

"You had better lie down at once," said the man's voice, "otherwise you will get cold."

I was startled by the voice. I had expected it to be the voice of a homeless wanderer, dispirited and coarse: whereas the voice was vigorous, clear-cut and almost harsh.

"Thank you," I said, "but I hate the idea of lying under those blankets."

The man laughed and said:

"It's your first time in a position like this? You are a foreigner? Of what country?"

"Ireland."

"A sailor?"

"A writer."

"Then you should be pleased at having the opportunity of a new sensation," he said in English.

I was still more surprised, for he spoke English perfectly.

"Perhaps I should be pleased," I answered, "but it's not really a new sensation. When I was young I experienced sensations far more sordid and repulsive. I was a beachcomber in Rio de Janeiro once, and that was really frightful."

"Nothing is frightful that one feels," he said. "The only thing that is really frightful is to live without feeling, to get so used to one's life that it leaves no impression, except one of boredom. Are you rich?"

"No. I am a poor man."

"Have you been rich?"

"Never."

"Take off your shoes and get under the blankets, otherwise you will catch cold."

While I was taking my shoes off he continued:

"I have been rich twice. The first time when my father died, and once after the war, when I myself made another fortune. The fortune that my father left me was lost in Russia, and I lost the fortune that I made myself in gambling. I do not think I shall make another fortune."

He uttered the last sentence in the tone of a man who had decided not to do something, and that surprised me very much.

"How did you make your second fortune?" I said.

"Steel," he rapped out, as curtly as a sergeant giving an order to a recruit.

I lay down and pulled a corner of the foul blankets over me. The stench was really frightful.

"Do you wish to sleep at once," said the man, "or do you like to talk?"

"Well," I answered, "I should like to know why you, who had two fortunes, one of which you made yourself in steel, cannot persuade society to offer you a better lodging."

"That is an amusing question," he said with a laugh. "The answer is equally amusing. This sort of life is my third fortune."

"Oh!" I thought. "Here is another of them."

For a few moments I thought the man was potty, but there was no confusing the clarity and sharpness and coldness of his speech with the rambling of a madman.

"I have done everything, as they say," he continued, "and having done everything, I have come to the conclusion that to live without effort or responsibility is the only mode of life that can give real happiness. Do you believe in God?"

"That is a difficult question to answer. God as a varying symbol of perfection seems to me consistent with the quality that we call rational in the human intellect."

"That is the nonsensical talk of a writer," he rapped out, "but what I want to know is do you believe in a God that will reward the good and punish the wicked in an eternal life after death."

"No."

"Then you must admit that my conception of happiness is right."

"It does not necessarily follow."

"Why?" he cried fiercely.

"Because I believe that life and death are also symbols, just like God, of the attempt which our human intellect makes to detach itself from universal ignorance. Neither life nor death exists except in our intellect."

"That is nonsense," he said curtly. "You must remember that I once made a fortune in steel. In steel. It is a very hard substance. You would never make a fortune in steel, because your mind is too confused."

"Perhaps it is, but at the same time this confusion

enables me to form a higher conception of human happiness than yours."

"What is your conception?"

"The degree of the individual human being's happiness is in direct ratio to the degree of his struggle against his environment."

"To what purpose is this struggle if God and life and death are merely symbols?"

"Towards achieving omniscience."

The man laughed and said:

"You are a funny fellow. I am glad I met you, especially here. It proves to me that I am right in choosing this manner of living. When I was a rich man I never met funny people like you, or when I did meet them they were not funny, because they wanted some of my money, and so they flattered me by trying to say what they thought I would like to hear. People say what they think is true only to those whom they consider their inferiors. I also never had time to say what I thought was true, or do what I thought was really funny, because the terrible tragedy of the rich man is that he never has any time to do what he really wants to do. He is either busy keeping what money he has or making more. Very well. Now I have plenty of time and I do everything I want."

"Then you are being false to your philosophy of happiness."

"How?"

"By doing anything at all."

"I see your point; but I do at least as little as possible. I am on my way to the East. I shall arrive there on foot all the way if possible. I shall never come back. It is easier to live without effort there than in Europe. Europe is a mad continent. It is approaching its doom. I mean its inhabitants."

"Perhaps."

"There is no perhaps about it," he cried, drawing the filthy blankets up about his ears. "There is going to be a great war, during which groups of airmen will seize power in the different countries. There will be a new sort of feudalism, only the aristocracy will be barons of the air instead of the earth. The flying barons. As in every other sort of feudalism there will be continual quarrels among them, until all cities are in ruins and civilization will completely disappear. We are approaching the end of the period of civilization which has lasted during the last three or four thousand years in varying stages of development. Man will return to his natural state of barbarism."

"You believe in Anatole France's theory of civilization," I said.

He turned over on his side, discharged wind, and said with a yawn:

"There is no hope for humanity. There is no God. That is all."

"What about the Russian experiment?" I said rather angrily.

He sat up, laughed very heartily, and cried in his sharp tone:

"That is the greatest joke of all. The Russians are savages. It is a great joke that they should be entrusted with the last attempt of our civilization to create a God.

Bah! They could never make a fortune in steel. I am on my way to the East. Good night."

He fell asleep almost at once, snoring very heartily, much to my disgust. I could not overcome the nausea aroused in me by the stench of the blankets and of the cell, so I lay awake brooding in a frightened way on the Godlessness of the universe. In spite of my antagonism to the crazy fellow's ideas, I heard the whine of aeroplanes swooping down from the clouds on cities and then the crash of bombs, the wail of millions waiting for their doom. Then an awesome silence reigned over the earth, broken only by the snoring of the man beside me.

In the morning a policeman took him from the cell. I heard him ask for bread and being refused. He who had made a fortune in steel could not persuade a policeman to give him a crust. Later I was myself released, and having paid a small fine, I took the boat back to England *re infecta*, as even Julius Cæsar had to report at times.

### VIII

AFTER this brief diversion I continue my expedition into Brittany in search of truth, but with diminished hope of being able to arrive at it. The more I write of this distressing book, the more I am convinced that it is impossible for a writer to put down even a stockbroker's conception of the truth about himself. What ho! The fact is that he has a tendency to become a Methodist inveighing pretentiously against his own sins, unless he is a pompous fellow of small wit who should really have been a stockbroker. Here goes, therefore, in an effort towards finding some virtue in myself. Otherwise this Jeremiad may make me despair of the future; death from a malicious itch in a workhouse bed instead of that slippered old age in an armchair, with a pipe and wineskin and the love of good friends, for which we all hope.

I arrived at Quimper in the early morning on the train from Paris. Then I took the omnibus from Quimper to Concarneau, where I luckily found lodgings at Eveno's tavern on the quays. To my sorrow, I discovered that the good Eveno, that jovial fellow of immense girth, had been called to the bosom of the Lord in the previous year, following a surfeit of absinth. His widow Armande, almost the equal in girth of the deceased Louis, gave me a room overlooking the harbour, and then invited me downstairs to the bar in order that we might renew our acquaintance of three years previous over a glass of something stimulating. To her manifest astonishment I ordered a tumbler of still mineral waters.

"What!" she cried, throwing out her arms. "Has the world come to an end?"

"It has very nearly come to an end for me, my dear Madame Eveno," I answered, "unless I stick to mineral waters."

"Ah!" she said. "You foreigners have a dreadful habit of drinking unreasonably. You go on a binge and then you suffer remorse. Why don't you learn to drink moderately? Then you would understand that the good God invented wine for your pleasure and happiness and not as a drug to be taken in time of sorrow or weariness.

It is obvious that you have been making a fool of yourself since you were here last. Go for a walk along the seashore and come to your senses. Are you ill?"

"I have been ill, but I am nearly all right again, except that my throat is sore and I still have a rash on my lips."

"Very well!" she said. "Go for a walk and when you come back I'll have something for your throat and also for your mouth. We must make you presentable to the ladies as well as healthy. Be off."

Her kindness and her exuberant energy excited in me that feeling of enthusiasm for life that is always produced in me by these two qualities. I went to look at the town, certain that I had chosen the best place in the world for my recuperation. It was a day of glorious sunshine and the beautiful harbour was crowded with tunny boats, just returned from their cruise in the Spanish seas. They lay close together, their tall masts and tunny rods intertwining as they reeled on the swell made by some passing tugboat. Their hulls and sails were all the colours of the rainbow and the sunbeams playing on them reproduced their fancy colours in the depths of the white, still waters of the harbour. Their crews, dressed as gaudily as the boats, in red and blue and orange, sat on deck, singing or playing accordions, while some paddled themselves ashore to get drunk, standing in groups in the prows of their little paddle-boats. On the pier there was a crowd of women in Breton costume, shouting out the current prices of tunny fish to the approaching fishermen. A smaller crowd, down at the end of the digue, watched a tunny boat discharging her cargo. The stiff corpses of the fish, neatly disembowelled, looked like short, fat torpedoes, as they passed from their perches under the tarpaulin on the boat's deck to the lorry that was to take them to the factory. Beyond the entrance to the docks, other boats approached under full sail, gorgeous in the sunshine. On the left lay the old town, within the fortifications that Vauban had built. On the right stretched the Atlantic, with the Glenans islands dotted on its surface in the misty distance.

"How good this life is!" I thought with joy as I walked along the seashore to the right. "Here all is in harmony. Men foraging in the sea for its fruits, sailing their beautiful boats and bringing home rich spoil. Women waiting for their men. Taverns to cheer with their wine those who have returned from dangerous toil and wish to make merry. What gentle simplicity and graciousness!"

The tide was going out and I left the road to scramble along the rocks that were still wet with the brine that had recently covered them. At every few steps I halted to listen with delight to the murmur of shell-fish, the low hiss of the tide flowing among the yellow, swaying weeds and the distant cries of children playing in the surf upon the strand below the Grand Hotel farther to the right. The salt smell of the sea entered my lungs and then flowed through my being with healing power, to scour the taint of cities from my blood. I climbed to the top of a great rock and there I stripped my feet and my body upwards from the waist. I sat and basked in the sun and realized that I was content after a long period of unhappiness.

And then I remembered how I had sat on this very

rock three years previously. That was in the early autumn of 1930, shortly after my return from the Soviet Union. I shuddered involuntarily at the memory, for indeed it is always terrifying to find oneself after a lapse of years on the same spot of the earth's surface; returned thither unwittingly. And as a consequence, the sun's splendour at once assumed a malign quality. The cries of the children became eerie, like the crowing of distant cocks on a quiet afternoon; which cries have in them a note of dismal warning. Insecurity!

How easy it is to see past mistakes when one feels insecure! Now, as I sat on the rock, I understood that probably the greatest folly of my life was the flippancy of my conduct during my visit to Russia, and the criminal mockery of the book which I wrote on my return about my experiences and impressions in that work-shop, where the civilization of the future is being hammered out by the gigantic labour of heroic millions. I had crossed the Soviet frontier into Poland in a state of exalted enthusiasm for all I had seen and determined that I would do everything in my power to excite all whom I could reach by word of mouth or by writing to help in the task of winning over humanity to the Soviet cause. I reached Berlin still in that state. There I met Heinrich Hauser, who has now, I am told, become a propagandist for the doctrines of Adolf Hitler. I was surprised at the coldness with which he received my eulogies of Russia, and then, while we were driving in his car through the square that was once Kaiser Wilhelm Platz, I remarked that it would shortly be re-named Red Square. He turned on me savagely and said:

"No, it will soon be called once more Kaiser Wilhelm Platz."

I made no reply, but I felt that in some way he had become an enemy; and then I reached London, where I met P. R. Stephenson, who was at that time running the Mandrake Press. He incited me to write about my experiences in Russia. * * * * * * * * * * * *
* * * * * * * * * * * * * * * * * * * *
* * * * * * * * * * * * * * * * * * * *
* * * * * * * * * * * * * * * * * * * *
* * * * * * * * * * * * * * * * * * * *
* * * * * * * * * * * * * * * * * * * *
* * * * * * * * * * * * * * * * * * * *
* * * * * * * * * * * * * * * * * * * *

My friend Albert Sachs of New York was staying there at the time and he joined with Stephenson in inciting me to write a thoroughly propagandist book. I set to work, firm in the intention of writing something that would please them; but for some extraordinary reason the book became maliciously satirical from the very first page. My friends, as they read the manuscript, became suspicious and then frankly hostile.

"Why, it's a goddam reactionary piece of work," Stephenson said. "What's the idea?"

The gentle Sachs said it was amusing but more likely to give comfort to our enemies, the bourgeoisie, than to our friends. I got angry with them and maintained that it was by no means reactionary and that I could only write as I felt. It was more subtle, I maintained, to begin by being flippant and then to finish in a heat of fanaticism.

"Very well!" said Stephenson. "Go ahead. Do it your own way."

I had done about half the book at the cottage when my agent telephoned me one day to say that he had sold the dramatic rights of *Mr. Gilhooley* to New York for a large sum of money. I immediately ceased work on the book and went to London. Having made provision for my family for a year, I decided to go on a long journey, during which I hoped to forget the immediate past and recover my old enthusiasm for work. For about a week I toyed with the idea of going to Malaya, and indeed I left London with the intention of arriving somewhere in the East; perhaps even in China. But I got no farther than Brittany.

It happened this way. I landed at Saint Malo at six o'clock in the morning, accompanied by all my kit. I took an ancient taxi, piled my luggage into it and told the driver, when he asked my destination, that I was bound for Vienna.

"Vienna?" he said in astonishment.

"Yes," I said casually. "Drive me to Vienna."

"But that's in Austria."

"Of course it's in Austria," I said. "You don't suppose it has moved to the Balearic Islands, do you? Drive me to Vienna. I have never been there."

"Impossible," he said. "Even if I wanted to go into a foreign country I could not do so. Why do you want to leave France? For what insane reason do you want to leave France and go into a Boche country, where life is unpleasant?"

"Very likely," I said, after a little reflection, "there is

some sense in what you say, but if I had any sense, or if I were prone to listen to sense, I'd not be here. Drive me wherever you please. Where am I now?"

In point of fact, I had merely a poor idea of my whereabouts, having got on the wrong train in London.

"You are in Brittany," he said, "and I happen to know a town that would suit you far better than Vienna."

"Take me to it," I said.

We set forth. It was then about half-past six in the morning and we did not arrive at Concarneau until late that evening, having crossed the Breton peninsula in our ancient car. The driver and myself were very much the worse for wear when we arrived, for we sampled every sort of drink that had ever been tasted in Brittany on the way. We lost our road several times, turned back, aside and went round about. We had long discussions and arguments with everybody we met and some very extraordinary adventures which I have quite forgotten, not being very sound in the memory when they occurred. In any case I found myself at the Grand Hotel in Concarneau, and there I stayed, having abandoned all idea of going either to Vienna or to Bangkok. As my friend Stroud would say, I saw clearly that one could be just as unhappy at Concarneau as at Bangkok, and quite conceivably as well able to think in one place as another, so why go farther?

I stayed at Concarneau for about a month, during which time I wrote a little more of my book about Russia, but not very much. Then I began to receive telegrams from a friend of mine who was in an untenable position on an island in Lake Constance. I moved on to Paris in answer to his frantic calls for help and then took the train to Constanz, where I arrived early in the morning. I spent the whole day wandering around the lake on ferryboats, stupidly trying to find his island and continually going astray, once as far as Zurich, or some such town in Switzerland. At last I discovered his island at nightfall, made my way to the hotel he had inhabited and found that my bird had flown. Where? I was told he had gone to London. I angrily returned to Paris and pursued him to London, where I found him at the counter in the saloon bar of the Plough tavern, immaculately dressed, as they say, in full evening kit, with a gold bangle on his right wrist and a young woman on each arm.

"What is the meaning of this?" I cried. "You wire me to say you are in a bad way on Lake Constance, on the point of foundering, so to speak, with all hands and I find you emptying the pigskin at the Plough, with all the appearances of prosperity. What's the meaning of it?"

He whispered in my ear that his circumstances had very materially changed in the meantime and that he was now commissioned to buy horses for the Venezuelan Government. I left him in disgust and went to my hotel, where I found a letter from a girl in New York, saying that she was ill and also in an untenable position. As if I were suffering from a mania for rescuing people, I decided to go to New York at once. Within a few days I sailed from Southampton on the *George Washington*, still carrying the unfinished manuscript of my book about Russia. I had grown to hate the thing. I had lost interest in Russia and in all experiments for the improvement of man's condition on this earth. I had fallen into a state of complete intellectual boredom, from which a journey across the Atlantic on a liner was not calculated to arouse me. My old unpleasant friend, melancholia acuta, had come to stay with me and there was no ousting the fellow.

Indeed, I am frankly puzzled to know why doctors recommend a sea voyage for those suffering from nerves, or recovering from an illness. For there is nothing in the world as boring as a sea voyage for an intelligent person; I mean a sea voyage in idleness. Certainly to work on a ship as a member of the crew is a splendid thing; but to loll about the ship as a passenger seems to me loathsome. Even in the company of a close friend I can imagine it would be a dull affair; but in the company of strangers, who are sure to appear to a bored person to be a vulgar lot of scoundrels, it is an unbearable agony. On the first day after leaving Southampton I wandered about the ship, hoping to find someone to amuse me during the trip, for I was in no temper for work. As always happens in such cases, I was seized upon by the greatest bore among the passengers, an American business man from the middle west.

As soon as he had collared me, he launched forth into a history of his life. He walked around the promenade deck ten times, while he described the early part of his career as a lawyer in Porto Rico. Then he edged me into the smoking lounge, ordered drinks and continued his career as a big business man in a middle western city. By lunch-time he had brought his story up to the commencement of his descent on Europe with his wife and family. I escaped from him at lunch to find myself at table with a sinister Australian business man who was making a tour round the world, " for pleasure," he told me with a scowl. He found the world, so far as he had seen it, a horribly mismanaged place, and he saw no hope for the future except in business men of his own calibre setting up dictatorships in the different countries. He had not laughed, he said, since he left Sydney eighteen months previously. He had no intention of laughing, he said ferociously, until he reached Sydney in six months' time. He swore savagely that he would never again take a holiday.

I tried to sneak out of the dining saloon without being caught by the American; but there was no escaping the fellow. He took me by the arm and introduced me to his wife, his daughter and his mother-in-law. We all went out on deck, where I was again forced to listen to the further adventures of the American, including the exact amount of money he had spent in Europe, the facility with which a crook could cash travellers' cheques in remote Balkan countries, the income he derived from his apartment hotels, his bank and his various other business concerns, the measures he was taking to ensure that his only daughter would be able to look after her money when she came of age. Then he told me to run along and amuse the kid.

The kid was a very hard-boiled young woman of nineteen. She proposed that we go into the smoking-room and drink beer. We did so and then she told me that the only thing that amused her was the recital of bawdy limericks. Otherwise, she was of the opinion that life was very wet. She was still a virgin, although she had often gone to bed with young men. She hung on to her virginity, she said, just to annoy the young men who wished to deprive her of it. She thought Europe and its culture were all bolony; but the middle western city in which she lived was still more wet and she looked forward to the winter with horror. She said that the first thing she would invest in on getting hold of her money was a clever guy, whose sole job would be to compose bawdy limericks. She'd fire him if he could not wake her up every morning with a new one. Then she left me to go to the cabin of one of the post office officials, who offered to share a bottle of French brandy with her.

After leaving her I picked up a Frenchman, who asked me in a very disagreeable manner whether I was a Belgian.

"Then," he said angrily, "you are a complete foreigner like the rest of the passengers."

"I certainly feel one," I replied.

He shrugged his shoulders and said:

"Naturally, one feels a foreigner if one is not French, but at least you speak a little of the language. That is already something. Never in my life have I seen such a ship. I am practically certain that I am the only Frenchman on board. I inquired at the bursar's and he told me so. There is, I grant you, a Swiss, but what is a Swiss? One can never be sure that a Swiss is not a Boche or an Italian. They do make a good cheese in that country, I must admit, but is it in any way comparable to our cheese? For a Swiss cheese it is something, but what is a solitary cheese compared to the immense wealth and variety of the French kitchen? And . . .

name of God . . . to think of the wines of France! Ha! ha! That is a day the good God did not waste, when he planted the first vine on French soil. And then . . . on this barbarous ship it is impossible to eat, drink, or make love. They have even committed the barbarism of placing me at table with a sort of an Italian, a sort of Sicilian, a Maltese no less, a wretch of a Syrian, a misbegotten son of a Jew, a fellow who insists on talking to me about music in most foul French. About music. He insists on talking to me about music. Then there is a Pole who has the effrontery to tell me, to tell me, a Frenchman from Orleans, that the Poles could have beaten back the Russians in 1920 without our help. To cap it all, I feel practically certain that I shall be forced to keep on meeting cattle of this sort until I reach France once more. But I can assure you, sir, that having spoken to my brother in their town of Washington and having visited their town of Chicago, about which one has heard amusing things, I shall return to France, never again to leave it."

"There is an Australian on board," I said mildly, "who has said the same thing about Sydney."

"Sydney," roared the Frenchman. "Where is Sydney?"

"In Australia," I said.

"Bah!" he yelled. "Australia! A barbarous colony of a barbarous empire. One is a fool not to have waited for the *Ile de France*, where nobody ever gets sober from one end of the voyage to the other. I am a fool. A damned fool."

"Do you know what Socrates said about fools?" I ventured to remark.

"I have no respect for philosophers," he cried, "with the exception of Descartes, who was a good Frenchman."

"I dare say you would have no respect for Socrates," I retorted, "for the reason that he would agree with your self-accusation of folly."

At that moment the ship lurched, hurling the Frenchman, who was on the point of lurching suspiciously towards me, and he was a burly fellow, into the bosom of a huge American war-widow, returning home from a tour of the European battlefields. I myself backed a few paces and collided with a woman, who told me, hot-foot on my apologies, that she recognized me from a photograph that she had seen in a Moscow newspaper, that her husband was an engineer working for the Soviet Government, that she liked living in Moscow because an engineer's wife in that city did not suffer the social disabilities she would suffer in New York, granting that she had the natural ambition, she meant in New York, of associating with her social equals, who were all so snobbish, she meant in New York, about the amount of money people earned . . . whereas in Moscow . . .

"Pardon me," I said savagely, "I have an appointment."

I locked myself in my cabin, opened my typewriter, took out my manuscript and determined to work. The crass fecklessness of all these people crossing the Atlantic on journeys they did not want to make, hating the places to which they had been, or to which they were going, without enthusiasm either for the future or for the past, should, I thought, excite me to eulogize Soviet Russia, where the future was glorious and unbounded enthusiasm the common attribute of the meanest citizen. Yet I could not write. On the contrary I found myself dreaming about a wild swan. I saw this wild swan fall wounded from the upper air into a pond where village geese were feeding. One of the geese, enamoured of his beauty, cared for his wound, fed him and sheltered him in her nest until he was well. But when he was well and Spring came on the air, the wild swan, indifferent to the goose's love, rose on his powerful wings and disappeared, leaving the goose disconsolate.

"Why be a goose? Let the geese and ganders of the earth waddle in their muddy ponds, plunging their beaks into the mire and excrement in search of gold, or God, or the perfection of their ephemeral institutions. Let them hiss and flap their shabby wings and peck to death their rivals, when they are beset by the base confusions born of their ignorance. Fly high, my soul, and when the icy hail has pierced the snow-white armour of your beauty, let subtle grace be your purse, full to overflowing with hypnotic rubies, to make soft your fall. But while you soar in sunlit splendour, the petty loves and hatreds of geese and ganders are no concern of yours."

Indeed! How could it be my concern whether one man or twenty governed this or that slice of the earth's surface? Why should I care if a ruler's head wore a royal crown or Lenin's cloth cap? My business being to watch and to sing without impartiality of man's thoughts and movements. And in the feverish turmoil of Moscow, labouring night and day for the construction of a world state, I saw only the British ambassador, calmly playing tennis with men of his staff on a lawn behind his embassy.

"Do you play tennis?" he said. "No? Then have a whisky and soda."

Between the calm dignity of the Old Order, courteous and smiling, indifferent to the turmoil outside the walls of its outpost in the capital of the enemy country, playing the silly game of tennis in white flannels, and the New Order training its red millions for the Old Order's overthrow, I must stand simply as a watcher, having no billet in either camp. To the one I was "rather a queer fellow." To the other "an individualist and therefore a suspicious character."

"Then let the geese and ganders fight it out," I cried, putting the manuscript away.

Nor could I write a word during the voyage, either about Russia or about my wild swan.

I arrived in New York to find a man from my publisher's office waiting to receive me, for America is the most hospitable country in the world to anybody whose name has ever appeared in print, unless it be in connection with what they amusingly call "moral turpitude.' Thus Maxim Gorki, one of the most talented living writers, was refused admission because he arrived in the company of a woman with whom he was in love but had not officially married. Not being accompanied by a woman I was received in a kindly fashion and interviewed by journalists, just as if I had been a famous gangster, or film actor, or designer of women's underwear. The customs officer ransacked my luggage in search of alcoholic drink and I was allowed ashore.

At once I became frankly terrified, for I found myself in a city where all movement is intensified to a degree that dazes a European. It is just like being swung round on a crazy railway, or looking down into the sea from the summit of a very high cliff. To a nervous man like myself, this experience becomes insufferable after a little while. And yet I was hypnotized by its novelty, its nightmare splendour. My guide hurried me from one place to another, so that I was quite beside myself after an hour or so; for we never had time to stay anywhere, having to spend all our time in getting from one place to another. All the other people in the city appeared to suffer in the same way, for I saw them hurrying in all directions, entering buildings of fantastic size, being swept up scores of stories in elevators, rushing along corridors, ringing bells, descending in elevators, rushing out of buildings, plunging into taxicabs. It was only by getting into a motor-car that one could draw breath and have time to look around one, or rather above one; for in New York one has a tendency to look upwards as in a cathedral, mesmerized by the height of the houses. I say, one escaped from speed to a certain degree by getting into a motor-car, since there were so many cars on the streets that each one could only rush along for a few seconds and then halt for several minutes until it was allowed to make the next rush. Speech was practically impossible, since the roar of the city's life was exactly like a jazz symphony, a "torch" symphony, to use that odd expression with which Americans describe a person singing about a hopeless love.

Indeed, the whole business seemed hopeless and inexplicable to me, for I could see no purpose in all this frantic movement. The people, although there were many millions of them, seemed to me the slaves rather than the masters of the fantastic buildings they had constructed. I have often watched for hours a tribe of ants scurrying back and forth about their ant-hill, feverishly busy with chores which seemed to me without purpose, but which were, no doubt, very rational to themselves. In the same way I watched the New Yorkers rushing about and felt certain that they were just as crazy as ants.

However, I concealed this opinion from my guide, since there is nothing so ill-mannered, apparently, as telling the truth about a foreign country while one is present there. One must wait until one has left it for some time and one's first impressions have become false. I simulated enthusiasm, therefore, in pursuit of good behaviour and exhausted myself in a show of energy as furious as that of any inhabitant of the town. I plucked out by the roots from my vocabulary all adjectives that were not of the superlative degree, wore my love on my tongue, made rash promises which I had no intention of fulfilling, turned night into day, never kept appointments, put on dog by asking for a slice of pig's cheek during a thé-dansant at the Biltmore Hotel, got drunk on pints of beer with debutantes of sixteen in speakeasies, visited the girl whom I had come to succour and found that she had married in the meantime and needed no succouring, enraged my publisher's staff by going to bed for two days in the house of a friend.

When I came to my proper senses after that long sleep, I found that I had already been ten days in New York. I felt like a man awaking from a slight attack of delirium tremens. My host, who was what they call a "big shot" in the American business world, felt rather hurt when in answer to his question I told him that I did not consider the continued existence of New York, as an inhabited city, necessary to the development of the human intellect.

"Don't think," he said, "because a temporary depression has just set in and you see white-collared workers selling apples at the street corners for a living, that New York is not still the headquarters of world finance. And take it from me, it's going to remain the headquarters of world finance."

"Very likely," I said, "but I am convinced that the future development of the human intellect does not depend on what you call finance."

"Say!" he said. "You're daft."

"On the contrary," I said, "I am quite sane, at the moment at least. In comparison with a New York business man my wisdom is even godly. Let us compare our mode of living. You are a typical New Yorker. Even judging you by New York standards, you are a very rich man. Now here you are, dining on two water biscuits and three prunes, which you are consuming with evident disgust. I, who am, to all intents and purposes, a penniless fellow, am sitting at your table, devouring your excellent food with a splendid appetite, drinking your good wine, which you have had imported at enormous expense, being privy to an offence against your own laws by so doing. And in order that you may enjoy the divine pleasure of eating two water biscuits and three prunes, you rush every morning to your office, you sit all day scheming and contriving in order to safeguard and increase your wealth, you carry on wars with your rivals, your nerves are constantly at an unbearably high tension, watching changes in the market, the production, the advertisement and the sale of your commodities and scores of other things that are quite horrifying to me. Just to come home and devour two water biscuits and three prunes. Do you think that you could persuade any man, sane or mad, that you are not a fool?"

"You're talking through your hat," he said. "I have power. That is what man loves most."

"The power to eat and drink and sleep and make love is the only power that is worth having, other than the power of reverie, which is normally contingent on the balanced exercise of the first named power. The wise man pursues wealth in order to satisfy his animal appetites and to lay in store a sufficiency for giving him leisure to enjoy the delights of his intellect. But you pursue wealth for itself, and that is where you and all New Yorkers of your convictions make such a ferocious error. You have the philosophy of the ant, which is a lack of philosophy. And for that reason, your magnificent city is likened in my mind to an ant-hill, whose millions of inhabitants toil feverishly at chores, to which there is no sane purpose. And for that reason also I am convinced that your tower of Babel is going to meet with the fate of the tower in the Bible. It will go down in history as a brilliant mistake."

"What you need," he said, "is to make a tour of the country and see our vast industries in process of . . ."

"Alas!" I said, "I have no time to do so. I

have to return to London to see a rugby football match."

"You're nuts," he said.

After that, there was nothing for me to do but leave, which I did on the following day, choosing an English boat for my return journey. Exhausted and disspirited, I had quite lost all ambition to finish my book by the time I reached London, but as a writer nowadays must produce something from time to time in order to live, I had to put an end to it. I ended it as I had begun, flippantly and without sincerity, except the shabby sincerity of the cynic. The result was that it amused those whom I wished to irritate and it displeased those by whom I wished to be respected. Instead of helping me to restate the purpose of my life and to get fresh vigour from that re-statement, it hastened the tempo of my disillusionment. It completed my loneliness; and while it may be true that the strongest man is he who stands most alone, that man must derive his strength from a greater love of humanity rather than from a paltry contempt for what is most beautiful in the mass efforts of his fellow-men towards the ennoblement of the species. It brought me to this rock on the Breton coast, a fugitive, as it were, from that eternal justice which pursues those who turn their backs on the struggle of life.

Woe! Woe to the infidel! For him the sun's luxuriant rays are spiked with poisoned barbs that turn the sweat begotten of his fear into a leprous rash.

## IX

For three days I lived very quietly at Madame Eveno's, and during that time I rapidly regained rude health, through the excellence of her table and the merry company of her household and of the splendid tunny fishermen who came to her bar for drink. All trace of my recent illness disappeared. I walked gaily about the town, and on the shore I sprang from rock to rock, with the litheness of an islander in my paces. Each day a glorious sun gilt heaven and earth with dazzling brightness. Its heat seemed to charm the blood of my spent youth back into my veins and I waited for the urge to begin work, almost like a young man waiting for the appearance of the maid with whom he is to fall in love.

On the fourth day I decided to begin. I sat down at a table before the open window of my room and composed myself to begin a tale that had been fermenting in my imagination for years. Immediately, I seemed to be struck a blow right on the crown of my head and my brain became completely numbed. The pen dropped from my limp hand, making a blotch of ink on the page. I bowed my head, shuddered and sat very still. And then, unconsciously I rose slowly to my feet, pushed back my chair and stared out through the window at the boats that lay moored in the harbour.

"*Aimons nous.*"

It was written on the broad stern of the nearest tunny

boat. Above the blue hull a yellow sail hung half furled on the mast and there were two out-curving tunny rods on either side the mast, tipping and leaning away from the rods of the neighbouring boats as the boat swayed on the tide. All the hulls and drying sails and masts and out-curving rods swaying on the tide. The rods and masts all gaunt and naked, like young trees stripped of their foliage, struck dead in a forest by lack of faith, leaning for succour on their mates and thrust away by contact with sterility like their own, their gaudy sails a mockery, whorish bags to catch the demon winds and scurry over the barren seas in search of truth.

On the shore beyond the harbour there was a rising field, its juicy grasses radiant in the sun; the dark earth's glossy hair; and on the hill above a cluster of great trees, their widespread, leafy branches skirting the rim of the sky, their bulky trunks moored safely by their multitudinous roots that grappled solid rocks and thick layers of spongy gravel. All safe and proud of their security.

"Oh, Christ, what have I done? What has died in me?"

I covered my face and wandered about the room, stunned by the unspeakable horror of the realization that I could write no more, that my soul was empty, stripped naked and barren, like the sere masts of the boats. Salt tears came to my eyes, but they would not rush forth. Salt without water; whitish salt grinning in the sun beneath the snout of a thirsty sheep in a shallow pool among the rocks. Oh, God! Could I only hear the rumble of sweet water leaping through its tunnel beneath a falling field and see its emergence from the dark brown clay in a little nook, round which in bygone days the people of my village had built a wall of stones, now covered with lichen? Could I only put my face beneath its silver spout and feel its soothing freshness on my eyelids? A well! A spring! The fountain of life! Only at the height of summer did it become silent, and then they put a dock-leaf to the spout and the trickle of water was caught in dippers by the waiting children, who sat about playing games and dabbing their naked feet in the little muddy pool in front, where cress was growing and funny insects fled from the prodding toes, humping their backs. Once when I sat there alone on an autumn day and the silence of the coming winter was already in the air, a she goat came and looked at me. I was struck with wonder by the queer wisdom in her yellow eyes and by the way she looked at me with lofty indifference and then walked away, with head raised and her supple ears twitching, listening and watching with the haughty calm of understanding.

"Yes," I thought. "That is the way a writer should look at life, with the calmness born of understanding, instead of wasting his frenzy on the destruction of icons and in teaching false philosophies to fools. Water runs. Blood flows through veins. Hearts beat. Tongues make song. All is the same and unchangeable. But beauty withers in sordidness and there is no pity for the fallen. There is less pity for the bird whose wings are broken and can no longer fly than for the worm which can only raise its head from its earthen hole and squirm in the sunlight. Lucifer was beautiful, but not as wise as the angels who bowed down and worshipped with their lips, while they laughed behind their masks. I have been a fool. What next?"

I sat down on the bed where I had slept the night. It was still undone. The clothes were tossed and the impress of my head was on the pillow. I stared at the pillow and then I remembered a sentence from *The Devils* by Dostoieffsky. It said that a man who has ceased to believe in God should logically end his life, there being no further purpose in continuing his existence. Suddenly that sentence appeared to me as a holy revelation and I willed to die; not because I no longer believed in God, but through a sensitive dislike for staying beyond my welcome. I felt at peace immediately and began to think clearly. So! It would have been the same, in any case, no matter how I had lived. My well had run dry. My tongue had become parched and there was no more song. I could no longer love and therefore I could no longer sing. Then why go on living?

"Yes," I thought coldly. "Death is the only means of escape. It is no use thinking that some time later I am going to change in character and be at peace in some quiet place, or by becoming absorbed in the casual amusements of my fellows, or by seeking satiety in the satisfaction of the appetites. It is far more dignified to determine the exact moment of one's going than to wait like a pauper for dismissal, delaying the moment when one has to leave the crumbs that fall from the table of life, at which one once sat as an honoured guest."

Now I remembered a writer called Padraig O'Conaire, who came to visit me at a cottage I had in County Wicklow. I talked to him for an hour or so in my little sitting-room while he drank a bottle of whisky, without seeming to get intoxicated by it. I drank nothing, but just sat and listened to his conversation. The man looked a dreadful wreck, almost in rags, his body twisted about like an old serf of the soil. Yet his ill-used face still retained some trace of his youthful beauty, and when he gave voice to some fine thought his eyes lit up with the fire of poetry. He seemed to know that death was upon him and to be inspired to a dark rapture by its imminence. The tragedy of his life weighed heavily on him and he spoke of the evil of his past; but he insisted that he had been driven to the excesses that had made him a homeless wanderer by loneliness, begotten of a lack of recognition.

"No matter what you do," he cried, pointing a finger solemnly at me, "make a home somewhere and stick to it. Have somewhere that you can call your own, even if it's only a mud-walled cabin. That is the important thing. Look at me and take warning. Don't smile. Don't think because you are young and healthy that you can play fast and loose for another few years and then settle down. To think like that will only bring you to the position I'm in. Build your nest and look after it when it's feathered. I'm strong yet, but I'm done for all the same, for there's nothing in here."

He stood up and put his right hand on his bosom.

"There's nothing in here," he repeated.

Then a devilish gleam came into his eyes and he grinned.

"I had a good day," he said. "Now I go the long road home. I had none on this earth, but I'll have one in the grave as good as any king. Good-bye."

He walked the fifty miles into Dublin, where he died two days later.

"Well," I said aloud, "I didn't take his advice about making a home on this earth, but I have at least free access to his royal couch in the bosom of the earth. When is it to be?"

When I asked myself this question, a rank smell from the dried bed of a small dock in front of the window came to my nostrils. Death appeared to be like that, a smelly, unclean state, full of worms and excrement. Following this thought came pictures of all sorts of death, by water, fire, strangulation, gunshot, poison; all unseemly and distorted. Then I felt a horror of death; a dreadful horror of that moment when life suddenly ceases; of that instant when the human soul becomes aware of everything, of the past as well as of the present. I shrank from the thought of killing myself, feeling certain that my body would never have the courage to suffer the indignity of reducing itself to that state of corruption.

I saw a trench behind Boesinghe one summer night in 1917. We were repairing a breach in the wall, filling sandbags and passing them from hand to hand, when suddenly duds began to fall. Somebody gave the cry of gas. Immediately everybody dropped what he had in his hand in order to put on his mask. There was a fellow beside me who began to tremble. I could only see him dimly through my goggles, but I felt his body hopping violently against mine, just like a frightened animal struggling in the arms of his captor. I myself was frightened, for I was unused to gas and I sat very still, not knowing what to do about the man who was hopping about. Then at last I reached out and nudged the man on the other side of me. He was a stretcher-bearer and he immediately dived across my legs and caught the man who was hopping. The fellow began to scream as soon as he was touched. He stuck his head into the muddy sandbags in the side of the trench. He clawed at them and screamed in a frightened way. Then the stretcher-bearer and myself dragged him out of the trench to the rear. His mask had been punctured by a splinter of shell and it was letting in the gas. He tore it off his face and tried to strangle himself with fright. His face was terribly distorted with fear and pain. I recognized him as a fellow to whom I had been talking that afternoon in a bivouac. He had said at that time that he was fed up with the war and that he hoped to get killed on the fatigue party that night. And yet when death came to him, he was more afraid of it than of the agony of living.

The horror of this recollection drove me as with a sharp whip from the desire to commit suicide. I sprang from the bed and went again to the table, where I sat down and prepared to write, with an almost savage determination. I called on all my energies, feeling that if I could not produce some words, no matter of what kind or on what subject, I could not put away that mad idea. But my hand trembled and I could only make crooked lines on the page like a child. My brain could produce no coherent phrase and yet it worked at feverish speed, concocting interminable pictures.

Then there was a knock at the door and I called on the person to enter. It was the woman who came to arrange my room. She was a dark woman, tall and lean, with a kindly face. The humanity of her smiling face was strangely soothing, and in the extraordinary way that a person under the stress of tense emotion reacts to mute sympathy, I at once passed from my despair into a state of wild gaiety. I began to converse with her, laughing and making jokes.

"Ah," she said, "how good it is to see a person happy like you. A happy person is a wonderful thing."

I laughed at the absurdity of the idea and I said:

"Do I look happy?"

"Of course," she said. "Your eyes are dancing. Look at yourself in the mirror."

I looked at myself and for a moment I saw that they were dancing, like the eyes of a man who has just heard wonderful news, like the eyes of a lover in the ecstasy of his passion, like the eyes of a poet in the fever of creation. But after a moment they glared back at me savagely, as if to say: "Ha! ha! You may fool others, but not yourself." And then I turned away and laughed again and said to the woman:

"You are quite right. I am fit once more. I have recovered from my illness. Now I'll go and have a drink. One must celebrate the return of one's health."

I dashed out of the room and began to descend the stairs towards the bar, but I halted half-way down and said to myself:

"There is no sense in running away now. In a few weeks I shall have no more money. Then I'll have to come to a decision. Why not now?"

Now, however, I could no longer see my eyes in the

mirror and I was able to believe in the deception of my happiness. My mind bowed before the vigour of my body. I ran down the stairs, but instead of going into the bar, I passed through a side door on to the quays. After all, I was shrinking from the execution of that gesture, struggling to maintain control over the desire to escape through alcohol from this fight with my conscience. I had said laughingly to the woman that I would go and have a drink to celebrate the return of my happiness, but I knew very well that if I did drink I would slip back into that state of feckless indecision which is the mark of a man who has no further "stomach for the fray."

On the quays there was a horrible stench from the dried dock on my right as I walked towards the centre of the town. I glanced at the foul, dry bed of the dock. Instead of the dock, I saw the bar of a tavern late at night, when the tipsy customers are being pushed into the street, and the barmen, with tired faces, are shouting: "Now, gentlemen. Time please." The floor is strewn with the ends of cigarettes and spotted with daubs of spilled beer. There is a horrid smell of rank alcohol on the air. The faces of the people look inhuman, bestial and depraved.

"Ah, yes," I thought, "that is so when you are tired and you have failed to get exhilarated by what you have drunk. Tut, tut, man, why all this drivel? Have a drink and cheer yourself up."

Forthwith I crossed to the pavement and sat down on the terrace of a café and ordered a glass of muscadet from the young girl who came to serve me. Even while she was gone for the drink, a voice still kept urging me to cancel the order and to go away, in order to continue the battle with my conscience. But another voice said in answer:

"Remember what that priest said in Rockwell about a teetotaller. He said that a teetotaller is like a dog with a muzzle. Everybody knows him to be a vicious fellow, who cannot be trusted to behave himself."

I felt very pleased with that remark of the good priest, but it started a train of sad memories. Now I could see the virtue of that priest, but at the time when he made the remark I felt very scandalized. I had been brought up with the horror of drink which is so prevalent among the poor in Ireland. Like most fears, I dare say that it had an economic basis; since even a rare visit to the public-house by the head of the family might mean hunger for the wife and children, or an inability to pay the rent, followed by eviction and the emigrant ship, or the still more dreaded workhouse. However, one cannot explain all there is in life in terms of bread and drink. It is more noble, even though it may be but partly true, to maintain that love is equal in importance to sustenance. A great deal of the Irish peasant's horror of drink is due to the debasing effect of drink on the character of our simple countrymen. The gentleness goes from the countenance. The manner is bereft of its courtly charm. The tongue can only utter foulness.

In that way, although the percentage of our people who abstain from the use of alcohol is greater than among any European people, the remainder who use it have gained for us the reputation of being a drunken race. And our drinkers, poor devils, have the air of criminals in their districts.

But there are two kinds of drinkers: the common gluttons who love alcohol for its own sake as a drug, and the jovial fellows who drink for the sake of company and gaiety. From my earliest days I had a horror of the first category and a passionate love for the second. My uncle was a drinker of the second category. I loved him very much, and even my mother, who continually deplored his character and held him up before her children as a solemn warning against the evils of intemperance, loved him more than any of her other relatives. For indeed he had all the virtues of Bacchus.

One night while I was sitting by the hearth with my sister, listening to a tale my mother was telling before going to bed, we heard singing in the distance. Mother at once paused in her tale and said:

"Holy Virgin! That's Pat singing. Be quiet, children. He's surely coming here and he's in drink. Your father mustn't hear him."

We all went to the door and opened it. It was quite late at night, but there was bright moonlight and the road leading to the village was distinct. On a hill about four hundred yards away we saw a horseman crouching on the neck of his horse.

"There he is," said my mother. "Oh, Lord! What'll we do with him? If your father wakes up and finds him there will be trouble."

Father was asleep, and since he had stopped drinking himself he had a horror of people who drank; nor would he allow any drink to come into the house, or indeed admit a person under the influence of drink. So my mother said:

"I'll throw something over my shoulders and go down to meet him. We must stop him singing. Wait here for me and be quiet."

However, my sister and I were afraid to stay behind, so we insisted on following her. As we hurried down the road, some of the village dogs began to bark, startled by the voice of the singer. My mother called out to him when we approached and he stopped singing at once.

"Who is that?" he said. "Ho! If it isn't my holy sister. There now. Sure you are the only person that loves me, Maggie, and aren't you kind to come at the dead of night to welcome me. I was drinking in the west, and I said it would be unnatural for me to go home without turning aside on the road to visit you. Give me your hand, you kind creature. And who are these with you?"

"Be quiet, Pat," my mother said. "Don't wake the village."

He chuckled gaily and whispered:

"I'll be as quiet as a mouse. Ho, my little darlings! And there you are, the two of you. All come out at dead of night to welcome your poor Uncle Pat. Faith, it's kindly natures you have. God spare your health. Twous."

He slapped the mare on the neck and she moved forward. I looked up at him timidly. He was lying forward on the horse's neck, one hand clutching the mane, the other hanging limply. He had lost his hat somewhere, and his thick, greyish beard was stained with the porter he had been drinking. He smelt of porter and his clothes were dishevelled, yet he did not arouse any unpleasant feeling in my timid child's mind, and I found that strange. Here was the man whom I was taught to regard as a desperate character, in the very commission of his depravities, roaming the island at night, singing drunkenly, and yet he said such pretty things and he made a child feel secure. My mother, however, continued to upbraid him vehemently in a low voice as she led the horse by the head to the house.

"Ah, sure, I know that, Maggie," my uncle kept saying in answer to her. "You fine, holy woman, I know all that. Sure, poor man, I know I'm a shame and disgrace to you."

Then he would sob in his throat and sigh heavily. But he spoke and he sobbed in such a heart-rending way that I felt he was in the right and that my mother was very wrong to upbraid him. And then we took him from his mare and led him into the kitchen. When he was seated comfortably in the corner of the hearth and my sister and I had taken off his top-boots, he changed his manner entirely. He looked about him slowly and then his humorous face became creased with silent laughter.

"You devil," my mother said. "You were fooling again and I thought you were ashamed of yourself. There is no hope that you'll ever mend your ways. Put on the kettle for some tea. Oh, dear, what sin did I commit to get a brother like you?"

My uncle suddenly slapped his thigh and began to giggle. He winked at me and I giggled too, although I felt certain that I was committing a sin by laughing with this desperate character who made my mother sob into the corner of her neckerchief.

"Sure I can't help laughing," he said, "at the funny thing that came into my head at this very moment. Though, it's how I should cry at it, now that I come to think of it."

Forthwith his face became doleful. Tears stood in his eyes, and he said in a most sorrowful tone:

"Maggie, my darling sister, I was just thinking how it will be in the next world. You'll all be up in Heaven among the angels, all dressed up very neat and sitting there, without a word out of you, listening to the music, and I'll be down in purgatory, or maybe worse, God forgive me for the mention of the place, in rags and dirty like a pig in a puddle, and being a mischievous devil of a man, I'll be shouting up at ye, claiming relationship, and all the other people there'll know that I'm a relation and ye'll be so ashamed of me, and all the same I'll take a horrid pleasure out of annoying ye, and that's the way it will be. Oh, God forgive me, Maggie, I'm an awful man."

Then again he began to giggle, flapping his fingers in front of his eyes. My sister and I were frightfully amused, and even my mother had to smile. Then my uncle gaily put my sister on one knee and myself on the other. He began to tell us wonderful stories, beginning with a fantastic adventure he had had earlier in the evening, with the ghost of a donkey that had belonged to a man in his village. Afterwards we had tea and pancakes which mother prepared as a special treat for us. When uncle went away in the small hours of the morning, I went to bed and lay awake thinking that it would be wonderful to grow up into a man like him. But at the same time, I was intimidated by the thought that he would have to stay so long in purgatory, being a nuisance to his relatives in Heaven.

Poor Uncle Pat! He had a most painful death, but he bore his last illness in the same laughing way that he had lived. I should much prefer to roast in purgatory with him, listening to his merry tales and perhaps quaffing an odd gallon of porter, that he would be sure to borrow from a kind devil, or whatever they have in purgatory, than to sit neatly in Heaven listening to the music with the whinging poltroons who seem destined for the upper regions.

And so, as I waited for the girl to fetch my muscadet, I reflected on the attractiveness of my bibulous uncle in comparison with the sober, hard-working and thrifty islanders who looked askance at him. He sowed not, neither did he reap. He squandered all he possessed, even cutting down the apple trees in his orchard and selling the wood for drink. Yet his life was gayer than the lives of his temperate neighbours. He was a noted figure in his district and his company was dearly sought after, owing to his wit and his gaiety. No matter how one could look at him, now that he is dead, in common with his thrifty and temperate contemporaries, he must appear to be a type superior to them. At the same time . . .

Ha! She put the muscadet on the little table in front of me. I looked up at her and smiled. How trim and pretty she looked in her elaborate costume that brought out the rounded contours of her full bust and of her shapely hips. There was a voluptuous gleam in her oval, brown eyes that looked into the distance. Her dark hair, peeping from beneath her tall head-dress, glistened in the sunlight and seemed to shoot little sparks from the fire of life that burned within her. Or was it the wine sparkling in the glass that gave her some of its joyous fire? She took my coin and went away with an indifferent phrase of thanks, obviously intent on some passionate recollection, of a song whispered in her ear, or of a lusty kiss upon her young lips.

It was the wine and the sun which made gay the liquor, for I saw it sparkle just as brightly after she had gone; and when I raised it to my lips and drank, its gaiety entered into me and I felt one with my uncle and with all men who sustain themselves against sorrow by its virtue. "Hey, boy, a stoop of wine." I stretched out my legs to their full length under the table, leaned back in my chair and folded my arms on my chest and thought:

"Yeah! I am tired of battle. Let me lie back and watch the labour of the human ants from pole to pole, with ribald mockery on my lips. Now I see their racket, the rapscallion hypocrites. Their gods and the virtues symbolic of their gods are contradictions of all that is beautiful and spontaneous in nature, which whirls in a bawdy dance of love from birth to death, from the juicy April rain to the silent winter snow. Hell roast their discipline. Whence comes this sanctimonious pride in the virtue of temperance? From greed and cowardice and a foolish belief that the wall can be surmounted.

But it cannot be surmounted. Man is no bridge between the ape and the superman. He is just a different sort of ape, a bridge between the lusty agility of the ape and the sagacity of the ant. An inventive brain that ministers to the body's pleasure, which pleasure whips the imagination to its dreams. That is his most useful quality. But to what use does he put it as a rule? He wastes it in a nonsensical struggle to make himself immortal, or different from what nature intended him to be, a little animal dancing on the earth's surface for a little while, to disappear in a little while, leaving no trace. Fornication, fighting and feasting are the only three pastimes worthy of a human being's consideration. If I ever again hear any man praise celibacy, or pacificism, or abstinence as a virtue, I shall knock him on the head. I have done my share of work. Another drink."

When I put my hand in my pocket to pay for the second glass I suddenly remembered the state of my finances. That changed the complexion of my mood, and I decided to leave this café in order to seek a place where drink was cheaper; for if this were to be my last wine-dream let it last as long as possible.

## x

I walked some way along the dock front until I found an obscure tavern, frequented entirely by working men. I entered the place, full sure that it would be as cheap as I could find. I sat down and ordered a glass of white wine from a plump wench who came to serve me. No sooner had I done so than a man hailed me from a corner.

"A glass of wine with me, sir," he said in English, raising his glass as he spoke.

I looked at him. He was a squat, broad-shouldered man, with a short neck and a powerful head. His hair was quite long and very thick, of a greyish colour. He had a strange face, with very heavy jaws, bronzed cheeks, high-boned and deep, blue eyes that were obviously dimmed and bloodshot through continual intoxication. His grey hair swept back from his high forehead in an arch, making his face look rather fierce, like that of a lion. He crouched over the table, his chin near his clasped hands.

I stared at him for a while, not a little intimidated by his appearance and by the arrogant way in which he had invited me to drink with him. When I had become accustomed to the abruptness of his interruption I said defensively:

"Have one with me instead."

"Rats," he said. "You want to make me move. Say, slave. Bring the gentleman's glass to this table."

The girl turned to him insolently and said:

"*Monsieur a dit?*"

"Damn your lingo," said the grey-haired man. "*Apportez le verre de monsieur a cette table. A toute vitesse.*"

He smacked the table with the palm of his hand and looked very fiercely at the girl.

The girl looked at me questioningly. In order to

avoid an argument, I got to my feet and moved over to the gentleman's table. He got up, bowed in an exaggerated fashion and said:

"Captain Timoney. At your service."

"Delighted," I said. "My name is O'Flaherty."

"What?" he cried, dropping down on to his chair suddenly. "Same country?"

"Very likely," I said, kicking back a chair, "if you mean Ireland."

"Astounding," said the captain. "I met another one yesterday. Not that I was impressed. As to you, that remains to be seen. The other fellow was an eye-sore. What is your regiment?"

"Haven't got one."

"What? No regiment? Haven't you served?"

"Do you mean God or Mammon?" I said, laughing.

The captain stared at me fiercely and then he wagged a finger and said in a sombre tone:

"Mark you. If you wish to be friends, no levity."

I shrugged my shoulders.

"Very well!" I said. "During the war I served in the Irish Guards."

"Shake hands," said the captain. "I wanted to make sure whether we could meet as man to man or otherwise."

"The fellow is drunk," I thought, as he gripped my hand in his mighty paw. "How unfortunate that I came in here!"

Having shaken my hand, the captain shuddered violently and broke into a snatch of song about an old shako.

"Do you know it?" he said.

I nodded and wondered how in heaven I was to get rid of him.

"This is an odd corner of the world," he continued, "and very likely my presence here needs some explanation. My presence here, sir, is not at all remotely connected with the universal quest for treasure."

He threw out his arms and added:

"Pieces of eight. Doubloons. Louis d'or. The necessary, in other words. It's got to be plastered on continually, if one wants to be in the race with a chance. We must get among the money."

He hit the table a resounding blow with his clenched fist.

"*Mais ça, alors,*" cried the waitress.

"Damn your lingo," cried the captain. "And you, sir?"

"Same purpose," I said, "if you mean to ask why I'm here. I came here to work."

He looked me up and down.

"Work," he said. "No hat, blue shirt, blue dungarees of a type that is not used by the local fishing gentry, no socks. I see the game. A painter, eh?"

"Next door," I said. "I'm a writer, or at least I was one until quite recently."

"Astounding," he said. "Shake hands once more. We're two of a kidney, hacks from the same stable. Hold on, though. Irish, did you say, and of the name of O'Flaherty. Are you the writer of that name, or are you just putting on dog?"

"That's very charming of you," I said with a smile, anxious to placate the crazy fellow.

He took up the glass the waitress had brought and held it in front of his face with comical solemnity. I raised mine in similar fashion.

"Top and bottom," he said, pulling back his shoulders.

We clinked glasses and were about to drink when the captain cried:

"The king, sir, and damn your eyes if you don't honour the toast."

He stood up and looked at me aggressively. I did likewise and we emptied our glasses.

"*Sont des fous, les anglais,*" whispered a fisherman in the far corner of the room to his mate.

The captain's quick ears heard the whispered remark.

"Fools, if you like," he cried arrogantly, "but our folly is the privilege of rulers. Chew that, fellow."

We sat down once more and I ordered fresh drinks.

"So far, so good," said the captain. "If you hesitated, I say hesitated, about honouring that toast, I should not hesitate, damn the word, I'm getting tongue-tied, or drunk very probably. I am drunk, dash it all, but I don't care two hoots. I say I wouldn't have hesit . . . blast the word . . . about cutting off the ac . . . she . . . ship. Just a moment."

He covered his face with his hands and remained motionless until the waitress brought us fresh drinks. Then he looked at me and said:

"I belong to the garrison Irish. I'm an *émigré*. They'd probably shoot me if I went back there. Not that I want to go back. Never went back anywhere in my life and have no intention of doing so. However, I'm a man without a country. So are you for that matter.

You're an outcast because of your books. They have condemned them in Ireland, have they not?"

"Some of them."

"Yes," he cried. "Put a beggar on horseback and he's sure to overstep the mark, or whatever the saying is. I couldn't endure it. Not to go back there and see beggars in the saddle."

It is difficult to get offended by the ideas of a drunken man, but it is very easy to get offended by his manner. However, in this instance, I got offended by the captain's ideas. Particularly, as I had brought myself only a short time previously to a state of philosophic Nihilism, in order to screw myself to the idea of committing suicide. The will to live in me was only too eager to avail itself of this insult to my common sense in order to destroy that idea.

"You are hardly being polite," I said, "considering that I am of the same race and class and approximately of the same opinions about the proper government of human society as those beggars, whom you say are now in the saddle of Ireland; that is, if you mean the Republican Government of southern Ireland."

The captain looked at me fiercely and replied:

"Sir, I do mean that Government, and I am sorry to hear a former Irish Guardsman give voice to these seditious sentiments, especially on foreign soil. On foreign soil, sir."

He waved his arms towards the fishermen, who were listening to us with amusement. I was beginning to get irritated with him.

"You talk like a character from Charles Lever," I said.

"A piffling lot of nonsense. On the contrary, it's you who are seditious. If you are an Irishman . . ."

"Don't mention the name in my connection," he cried. "I'm an Irish gentleman. There is a marked difference."

"Quite," I said. "I'm an Irish peasant, and as you say, there is a marked difference between us; but I am prepared to leave the question of superiority, from any point of view, as between the two of us, to a jury of dukes, whores, or Scotch Presbyterian parsons."

The captain struck the table with the palms of both hands and laughed uproariously. He yelled for more drinks.

"Shake hands," he cried. "You amuse me. You put on dog. The genuine *borzoi*. The absolute Irish wolf-hound. But tell me, point of general interest, why, if you are an Irish republican, does the Irish Republican Government ban your books?"

"Simply because I'm really a communist republican and that Government is republican only in name, being merely an executive committee that represents as closely as possible the economic ambitions of a community made up almost entirely of impoverished peasants. Even in the executive committee itself, the mentality of the impoverished peasant is strongly in evidence. It is only the personality of the president of that committee, Eamonn De Valera, that gives dignity and in some respects a world importance to the petty ambitions of the others. It's not he who condemns my books, but the others. As a matter of fact, his present economic policy was detailed by me in my novel *The House of Gold*, a book that was banned during the government of his predecessor."

"I can't follow you," said the captain.

"I can't follow myself," I thought, "but I mustn't let this fellow irritate me."

"I can't see," continued Captain Timoney, "how you can support De Valera and at the same time call yourself a communist republican."

"A communist pure and simple," I replied. "Allow me to explain. I am a communist because I realize that it is only through the state control of the production and distribution of social commodities that human beings can escape a revertance to barbarism and that this state control can only be effected through the dictatorship of convinced communists. That is beside the point, because the emergence of a world communist state, or revertance towards barbarism, has very little to do with Ireland. It may, however, have a little to do with De Valera. Ireland, either as an unwilling portion of the British Empire or as an independent republic, can have no bearing on the economic future of mankind, since the production of horses is the only respect in which it excels, from a world point of view, and the horse has been put into the ash-can by the internal combustion engine. At this moment, however, the existence of De Valera in Ireland, as the leader of the Irish people, is of considerable importance, for he is interfering with the possibility of British capitalism re-habilitating itself and therefore hastening the process of world revolution."

"This is getting beyond me," said the captain. "You're talking a lot of drivel. I'm a journalist, at this moment, for my sins, seeking fodder for an American magazine, a bull's eye view of European conditions, and

I should like to get the low-down, as they say, on the ideas of everybody connected in any way . . . damn this white wine. Funny thing, yesterday I had an argument with another Irishman, a benighted mist-on-the-bog type of Irishman, who is over here getting into contact with Breton nationalists. Bless the mark! He seemed to have an idea that the Irish have a divine mission to save the world from corruption, poverty, atheism, Communism, sin, which chiefly included sodomy and fornication, jazz music and negroid dancing. I forgot the Jews. He was hot on the Yiddish evil. But what struck me was that he thought De Valera was a poor fish, whereas you, who seem to have the same delusion about the divinity of the Irish mission, pox on these missions, you seem . . ."

"You are quite wrong," I interrupted. "I have no illusion about the divine mission of any race, least of all the Irish, in whose country there is very little of those raw materials, round which world power will centre in the future. These divine missions to rule the world and save it from numerous ills are becoming quite prevalent nowadays. They are believed in *ad nauseam* by the German and Italian Fascists, by the Irish nationalist fanatics, by the Russian communists and by the British Israelites. I believe that oil, electricity, steel and other mineral products will rule the world of the future. Divinity will stay where it always belonged, in the bowels of the earth. World power will rest with the inhabitants of those portions of the earth's surface, where these minerals are plentiful. But then, no one knows the future. There may be something hidden under the soil of Ireland that will revolutionize man's relation to the universe and make Ireland mistress of the world. Why not? But we have to wait for it, as the sergeant-major used to say."

"Now you are talking sense," said the captain, "although you are still a bit woolly. All this talk is in the air. Where do you stand on the vital matter? Are you for us or against us? The king!"

Again he got to his feet and I rose with him. We toasted His Majesty. Then we sat down once more. By now the fishermen were plainly laughing at us and taking no trouble to conceal their merriment.

"I insisted on that toast," said the captain, "because I know you are disloyal in your heart. That's what should be done to De Valera. He should be made drink the king's health at the point of the bayonet."

"I don't know whether he would do it or not," I answered, "as I don't know what his attitude towards the king may be. But I do know that he would not do so unless he wanted to do so. That is his virtue and his importance to his country. He only does what he believes is right, and nothing can move him; neither bribery, nor the better known forms of self-interest, nor fear can influence him. What Parnell did for his generation of Irishmen, De Valera is doing for this. Enslaved people need, more than anything else, a leader who can be steadfast without violence, stern without arrogance and just without cruelty. A lack of these virtues is typical of people who have been long enslaved or else who have not yet emerged from a state of barbarism. But people are quick to absorb the qualities of a great leader. He sets the pace for a new ruling class, or a code of social morality, whichever you prefer. He also puts to shame neighbouring people, who, having wearied of their greatness, allow themselves to be ruled by gutter-snipes, by common demagogues, whose eyes are centred on their pockets instead of being centred on the welfare of society."

"You are burking the question," cried the captain. "Are you loyal to the king or not?"

"My dear fellow," I said, "what is the king to me or I to Hecuba? A name blown by the wind, that carries the ashes of Ghenghiz Khan, of Alexander, of Ptolemy, of Julius Cæsar and of Solomon. My king is in my soul. To him I need not drink, nor do I ask others to drink to him. With my lips I drink to all kings external to myself, as to inferior beings that need an outward show of homage. But that is all the homage I give them, with the lips, a deference to the peoples of whom they are symbols."

"Then you are disloyal?"

"To what or to whom?"

"To the king and empire."

"You are silly. I shall back Australia in next year's test matches and England in next year's international rugby football tournament, De Valera as the likeliest winner in a contest for the most honourable statesman in the British Empire and Stalin as the only one of the world's rulers who is going to achieve greatness. I am not disloyal to the people of England, nor do I suppose for a moment that they care two hoots, as you would say, whether I am or not. But they do care about losing the Irish market for their manufactured goods, and that is the cause of their opposition to De Valera, who wants to build factories in Ireland and make the Irish self-sufficient, as far as manufactured commodities are concerned. The question of loyalty or otherwise is not to the king, but to the capitalists and financiers who rule England."

Captain Timoney eyed me for some time and then he said:

"You are a slick customer. Slave, give me a porto flip. I can argue with you when I have drunk a porto flip."

"*Qu'est-ce que c'est?*" said the waitress.

"Damn your eyes," said the captain. "Come along to my hotel. We'll have one there. I'm going to annihilate you in an argument. We'll meet the other fellow there too. I want to give him one or two stiff ones. Come along."

We left the tavern rather unsteadily, for I had to give the captain a hand. In the street he halted for a few moments to make a vague speech about "pieces of eight" and his intention of making a voyage in a tunny boat, in order to get the low-down on that sort of life for his American magazine. Then he gripped me by the chest, looked at me fiercely and said, winking his left eye:

"Do you think it's the right thing to live on England and then to be disloyal?"

"How do you mean? I don't live on England."

"Were it not for the English nobody would have heard of your work. You'd have been a drivelling little provincial writer in Dublin."

"Not on your life. Were it not for the Jews I'd probably be a very hungry writer. So would most writers who don't deliberately write tripe. Certainly, Gentile amateurs of literature have liberally praised my work in various countries, but one cannot eat praise, neither can one drink it. On the whole, it's only the Jews who think that an unpopular writer needs more help than praising him in a review, or getting his book from a circulating library, or borrowing it from a friend. In fact, my propinquity to England and the fact that I happen to write in English has been a great drawback to me. Had I written in French, Russian, or even German I should be a rich man now. At least I would have spent ten times what I have managed to spend. The English hate all Irish people who are not clowns for their amusement."

"Bitter fellow," said the captain. "Come along. You need a porto flip."

"On the contrary," I cried, as I hauled him along the street, "I am the least bitter of men. I'm not even bitter against my own fellow-countrymen, who would be more likely to shoot me than they would be to shoot you, in spite of the fact that you probably deserve being shot by them, whereas I have helped them considerably."

"Silence," roared the captain.

He struggled free of my support, staggered backwards and brought up against a wall, whence he glared at me in a menacing fashion.

"Remember I'm an officer and a gentleman," he growled. "I have overstepped the mark, I will admit. I've squandered my patrimony. I had to resign from my clubs. I'll admit everything. But I'm still a gentleman. Don't forget. Henceforth, don't you forget it. Come along."

He strode down the cobbled street, as straight as a rod, relieved of the unsteadiness begotten of his drunkenness by some frenzy of pride. I followed him, and presently we arrived at his hotel, where he planted himself in a corner of the lounge and ordered his porto flip. Three elderly Englishwomen who had been sewing there immediately got up and left, giving one to understand that they had not seen the captain for the first time. The captain, however, was indifferent to their disapproval.

"Waiter," he said, "*je veux causer avec Monsieur O'Donoghue.*"

"*Lequel, monsieur?*" said the waiter.

The captain waved his arms and threatened to overwhelm the waiter with a torrent of abuse, but I stepped into the breach and wrote down the difficult name for him. He went to fetch Mr. O'Donoghue, who arrived in a few minutes.

He was a tall, weedy man, with a furtive countenance and very black, curly hair. As I learned afterwards, he held a lectureship or a chair of some sort at a school or college of some sort, somewhere in Ireland. He was an authority, of some sort, on folk-lore, or folk-songs, or it might be folk-music for all I know, originating in Ireland, or some such country. At the moment, however, I was more interested in the extreme leanness of his neck, which he had the uncommon shrewdness to cover, as far as possible, with a very high starched white collar. He was dressed in black, except for his shirt, which was of the same colour as his collar. He smiled as he approached and took my introduction in a very civil way, but it was obvious from his eyes that he was of a character very eager to take offence. He struck me, furthermore, as a fawning and untrustworthy sort of fellow; a narrow-chinned, greedy-eyed, lop-eared rascal, with a slinking walk, like a nasty schoolboy coming up to his master to get slapped.

"It's a great pleasure to meet such a distinguished man," he said.

"Rats," said the captain. "Why don't you tell the truth? Yesterday, we were discussing this very individual's scribblings and you said most viciously that he is a living disgrace to his country. I remember that you . . ."

"Oh, please, Timoney . . ." began Mr. O'Donoghue in a very embarrassed fashion.

"Captain Timoney to you," cried that gentleman. "How dare you become familiar!"

"Mr. O'Flaherty," said Mr. O'Donoghue, "I beg of you to pay no heed to what he says."

"Shut up," roared the captain. "You said, in exactly the way I have mentioned, that the Irish should rise up in a body and burn him alive. Not that I care two hoots who is burned alive. But you said it. Come now. Have some moral courage, my man. Admit that you said it."

"One says many foolish things in the heat of an argument, Mr. O'Flaherty," said O'Donoghue.

"Oh, well!" I said. "What of it? A great number of the world's distinguished men have been burnt alive, hanged, beheaded, crucified and poisoned. Indeed, I regard it as a compliment that you and presumably many more Irish people wish to burn me alive. You don't appear to be the type of man who would do it on your own initiative and without assistance."

"You mean to insult me," he said, bridling up as I had expected he would.

In fact, I wanted to be offensive to him, in order to make him voice his real opinions.

"You can't expect me to feel kindly towards a man who wants to burn me alive," I replied. "Especially as I have never heard of you in my life."

"You have never heard of me?" he cried, quite losing his temper and becoming venomous. "Let me tell you that my name will live in the history of my country when you and your filthy books are forgotten."

"That doesn't interest me," I said. "However, I'd like to know why you consider my books filthy."

"They are obscene," he cried. "You defame your nation. You are one of a long line of degraded writers bought by the English to defame the Irish race."

The captain slapped his thigh and roared out laughing. I myself laughed, and although I felt hurt in spite of the ridiculous manner of Mr. O'Donoghue, I said gaily:

"I was once accused by the editor of a provincial newspaper of having sold my country for a lump of hairy bacon. Are you referring to that?"

"Damn my eyes!" cried the captain. "I'm as pleased as Punch to see you two getting at one another's throats. It proves that I'm right about the country inevitably going to pieces once the gentry were expelled."

Mr. O'Donoghue at once turned on the captain like a wild-cat and proceeded to tell him in most passionate language about the misdeeds of the Irish gentry. I was astonished that such a paltry frame could house such anger, and I was deeply impressed. The man's anger imparted itself to me. Although I remained offended by him, yet I felt a strange kinship with him, a kinship begotten of the hatred with which he was inspired. His passion had transformed his shabby countenance. He had ceased to be himself. He had become the mouthpiece of his race. I felt that I too was one of that race, that their passionate hatred was also mine and that its intensity made it beautiful. I could see why they were angry with me, believing that I did not appreciate their sufferings, or the struggle they were making to overcome their torturers. They believed that I mocked them, instead of fighting side by side with them and using my voice to state their case before the world. They believed that instead of singing them on to victory and peace I was harrying them with gibes and ill-timed criticism of their defects.

And yet . . . I suddenly leaned back in my chair and asked myself what it had all got to do with me. Let them argue. I must only listen and reproduce their passions. What would be the use of taking sides with the Irish peasants against the Irish bourgeoisie, or with the Russian communists against the bourgeoisie of the world, or with the English imperialists against the Irish nationalists, or with the believers in Jesus Christ's divinity against the believers in the Marxian theory of history? Leave all, take up your cross and follow me. All passion is beautiful, whether it is hatred or love. But how cold it is standing in the wings, watching the miming of the actors! He said he was a man without a country, but I am worse, for I am a man without the right to love or hate.

I got up, made a trivial excuse and left them. They were too intent on their argument to notice my departure.

I hurried back to my lodgings and locked myself in my room.

"Now for it," I said. "This has gone far enough. It might as well be now as later. Life has gone past me, leaving me stranded. The only thing to do . . ."

There was a knock at the door, calling me to lunch.

## XI

I LUNCHED with the family, and while I carried on a gay conversation with Madame Eveno's young nieces, inventing fantastic stories for their amusement about a fictitious Monsieur Pernod-Fils, I brooded on the idea of suicide.

Did I have the right to put an end to my life, considering that there were other human beings depending on me for support? In answer to this question, I put forward the theory that a sudden death, like suicide, sufficiently spectacular to be given a lot of space in the press, might draw such attention to my work as to effect a large sale for it over a period of a year or two; after which, of course, it would be forgotten, except by those who really liked it. By means of this ephemeral notoriety, my dependants would be able to rake in enough money to keep them for some years. However, I was inclined to doubt the efficacy of suicide as a means of drawing attention to a writer's work, or of intensifying his importance in the minds of newspaper readers. As I described the daily bath of Monsieur Pernod-Fils and how seventy-seven naked negresses poured gallons of choice champagne over his head, while skilled eunuchs massaged his limbs, I recalled the fate of various writers of note who had ended their lives in this manner during recent years.

The Russians I decided to omit, since suicide in that country has been, until quite recently at any rate, a sort of privilege of the intellectual class, whose attitude towards it was somewhat like the attitude of hearty young fellows of my generation towards a certain disease. In order to be regarded as a man, one must have had it at least once. In the same way, I suppose Gorki did not feel really grown up until he had put a bullet through his lung. Nor did Mayakovsky consider, I suppose, that he was acting counter to what he preached when he suddenly decided that he had had enough of the machine age about which he was so enthusiastic in his verses. Run short of ink, Essenin used blood from his artery and snuffed out his life in the process. We in western Europe take life more seriously, and I feel certain that it would be considered bad taste for a man to draw attention to himself by such drastic methods. If a maiden aunt tore open her bowels on the doorstep of a neighbour whom she suspected of ill-treating a cat, it would merely harden the public against cats and against those who make a fad of protecting feline interests.

However, I recalled the case of Peter Warlock, the composer, who put an end to his life a few years ago. The musical public paid considerable attention to his work for a few months after his death, and as far as I can remember, it was even broadcasted. On the other hand, the violent death of Darrell Figgis did no good to the work of that useful Irish writer. Very likely the public felt that he could not possibly have any grudge against it, since it had been kind to him during his lifetime. It was only in the case of writers like Mary Webb, whom the public had allowed to starve during her lifetime, that death loosed the mob's purse-strings, gave a friendly tongue to the critics and even made statesmen forget for a moment the economic development of Abyssinia in order to encourage English literature. But then her death was not effected by her own hand. It was the hand of God, meaning in her case the hand of the public which had let her starve.

But could I justifiably hope to meet with a similar fate? Have I got a grudge against the public? As I continued to describe the amazing adventures of Pernod-Fils while preaching Buckmanism to a horde of Chinese bandits, I had to admit that I had no grudge against the reading public. Considering that I have always treated it with the contempt which it deserves, it has been immoderately kind to me. After the first ecstasy of being able to express my ideas in writing had given way to a calculated scheme for making money out of writing, I cast about for a trick that would draw the attention of the public. At that time I was living in Oxfordshire in a cottage belonging to A. E. Coppard. I had as neighbours, besides Coppard, two other writers in the persons of J. B. Priestley and Gerald Bullett. It was during an evening at Priestley's house that I thought of trying out my trick on the public.

There were present Coppard, Bullett, Priestley and myself. Coppard was at that time living in a hut in a wood, quite alone, except for a tramp who lived under an oil-sheet a hundred yards away. It was then Coppard's ambition to be able to live comfortably on fifty pounds a year, accounting for all expenses and responsibilities. In order to do this, he told us, he was subsisting on vegetables, fruit and such soups as can be purchased in tins. Raw carrots he found to be most nourishing and inexpensive. Priestley, who is a humorous fellow, appeared to be deeply impressed by this idea of Coppard's.

"There's money in that," he said seriously.

"In what?" said Coppard.

"In carrots," said Priestley.

"Money in carrots," said Coppard.

"Yes," said Priestley. "You should tour England with the carrot idea."

Coppard seemed inclined to be offended by what he evidently regarded as ill-timed levity on the part of Priestley, but the latter proceeded to elaborate his theory in a very polite way, claiming that in the tremendous competition to which a writer of the present day is subject, spectacular conduct of some sort is necessary to draw attention to one's talent. The mountain, even if it wanted to go to Mahomet, sees a horde of Mahomets claiming its visit, so it stays put and the Mahomets have to crawl up its sides the best way they can. I thought his reasoning profound and I dubbed him a very shrewd man in my own mind. I walked home part of the way with Coppard, who tore at his curly black hair with his hands and cursed the bourgeoisie, with special reference to those who have schemes for tickling the mountain's rump and so making it roar out: "He is a man of genius. I'll make him a best seller." I agreed with him, but decided that I would have a shot at tickling the mountain's rump on my own account.

Priestley at this time was writing *Figures in Modern Literature* and Bullett had just written a book about Chesterton, or it might have been Shaw. I thought it might be a good thing for me to write a book about Pope Clement VIII, the weeping Pontiff who executed the Cenci in order to get hold of the family boodle. I would prove him a saint and thus win favour with the Catholic mob, both in my own country, in England and in America. The fellow was sufficient of a scoundrel to make his sanctification amusing from my point of view, while the Catholics would be pleased with my conversion to the right way of thinking. * * * * * * * * *
* * * * * * * * * * * * * * * * * * * *
* * * * * * * * * * * * * * * * * * * *
* * * * * * * * * * * * * * * * * * * *
* * * * * * * * * * * * * * * * * * * *
* * * * * * * * * * * * * * * * * * * *
* * * * * * * * * * * * * * * * * * * *
* * * * * * * * * * * * * * * * * * * *
* * * * * * * * * * * * * * * * * * * *
* * * * * * * * * * * * * * * * * * * *
* * * * * * * * * * * * * * * * * * * *
* * * * * * * * * * * * * * * * * * * *
* * * * * * * * * * * * * * * * * * * *
* * * * * * * * * * * * * * * * * * * *
* * * * * * * * * * * * * * * * * * * *

In Dublin I worked out the plan of *The Informer*, determined that it should be a sort of high-brow detective story and its style based on the technique of the cinema. It should have all the appearance of a realistic novel and yet the material should have hardly any connection with real life. I would treat my readers as a mob orator treats his audience and toy with their emotions, making them finally pity a character whom they began by considering a monster. Then, having put my tongue in my cheek, I returned to England with my wife and two bicycles. We cycled about the southern part of England while I wrote the novel. A good deal of it I wrote on the beach below the village inhabited by T. E. Powys, near whom we lived in a tent in a damp spot at the back of an old vicarage. While there, I had many lengthy discussions with Powys about the mountain and Mahomet. He insisted that the Government should stand between a literary fellow of worth and the indifference of the mountain, by giving the literary fellow of worth a turkey and a bottle of good burgundy once a week. Otherwise, he thought, the farther away the mountain kept, the better for the literary fellow of worth. Strong in the conviction that I was going to move the mountain by my novel, I disagreed with him and insisted that the literary fellow of worth should devour as much as possible of the mountain, even though he should have to begin, like Shakespeare, by holding its horses' heads at tavern doors. I cycled back to London and finished my book under a tree in Regent's Park. It had more or less worked out according to my specifications and I had no doubt about its effecting its purpose.

Its publication proved that I was right. The literary critics, almost to a man, hailed it as a brilliant piece of work and talked pompously about having at last been given inside knowledge of the Irish revolution and the secret organizations that had brought it about. This amused me intensely, as whatever "facts" were used in the book were taken from happenings in a Saxon town, during the sporadic Communist insurrection of about nineteen twenty-two or three. My trick had succeeded and those who had paid little attention to my previous work, much of it vastly superior, from the point of view of literature, to *The Informer*, now hailed me as a writer of considerable importance. In other words, the mountain had moved. And yet, perhaps Powys was right and that it would have been better for me if the mountain had not moved. If it moves too near one, there is a danger of being overwhelmed by its mass.

Certainly, I thought, as I told of the great success achieved by Pernod-Fils when he sang the *Stabat Mater* in the Vatican choir, it must have overwhelmed me, if I was now really contemplating the thought of suicide. The bright eyes and the merry laughter of Madame Eveno's nieces, together with the exhilaration produced by the wine I had drunk and which I was continuing to drink, made such a thought rather fantastic at the moment; so I decided to put it away until the evening and to enjoy fully the few hours that remained to me. Indeed, not for a long time had life appeared so beautiful and so pleasant. Like a man who pays his last shilling to see a film of luxurious living, with love and happiness as the reward of the actors at the end of the piece, the barren despair of the future intensified the pleasures of the present. The man in the cinema, while he is watching the exotic happiness of those on the screen, is hypnotized into forgetting that he must shortly march out into the dreary cold, to wander the streets all night, hungry, homeless and penniless, unless he obeys that suggestion that has been haunting him and throws himself into the river or under the wheels of a passing vehicle. In the same way I abandoned myself to the gaiety of my thoughts.

Wine had given me courage and the idea of death was no longer terrible. Conscience died. It did not matter whether one made provision for one's dependants or whether one left them to starve. The idea that one owed any duty to society appeared fantastic. One's work, or any merit that it might have, was a delusion; of no more importance than the journeying back and forth of an ant, or the rolling of a wave to a sandy beach. Homer's Iliad was of no more consequence than the laughter caused by my story of how Pernod-Fils, disguised as ex-King Amanullah of Afghanistan, read the whole of Gibbons' *Decline and Fall of the Roman Empire* before a meeting of the United Literary Societies of North Carolina.

In a paroxysm of satiric joy, as I smelt my glass of brandy, after the women had left me, I thought of the time when I was impressed by my own importance to humanity; how this most strange of all forms of insanity, the mania of genius, led me to imagine that I mattered in the universal scheme of irresponsible matter. Ho! ho! My jolly boys! What of the others one has seen? I was always able to laugh at myself, even at my worst; but I never forgot that the universe, in a certain number of millions of years, will have swollen to twice its size and then will burst, annihilating, together with all the various manifestations of man's genius, even the most trifling excrement of the tiniest insect. On the bottle was written the word "Trinc" and very little else can possibly matter in this world of dissolving matter. Before it dissolves, during the paltry moments that one inhabits it, during this drunken stagger that is life, the chief duty of man is to feed the fantasy with liquor and to love. To love and its natural outcome, to make love; to make love and to fight all who say nay.

God's wounds! How much easier it is to live among one's fellows, if one has an aptitude for hatred! "Long-haired preachers come out every night, to tell you what's wrong and what's right." Back again to this philosophic Nihilism. There is nothing in it. It even sours the effect of wine. To detest those who hate is just as bad as to hate. One must love even those who hate. Love everything and everybody. It is all a dance. Here come the merry fishermen all drunk. Drink with them. Hey you! Drink with me.

Making a rasping noise with their wooden clogs on the sawdust-covered floor, the crew of a tunny boat staggered into the room, followed by a little boy who was carrying an oar. They sat down at a table beside mine and we all shook hands, shouting uproariously. All fine men, who had filled their purses in the Spanish seas. Sea salt was on their tongues and they cried for wine. More wine and song and then again more salt and the wind singing in their sails.

"To hell with the bourgeoisie," one man cried, striking the table. "Last winter I made a trip to Leningrad and I saw things there, my friends. In that country the children are looked after. Here in France it is anarchy. The bourgeoisie takes everything and there is no provision made . . ."

"Shut up, Ernest," said his mate, hitting him a punch on the chest.

They all began to shout about the bourgeoisie and about the Russians who make provision for children, and then a man caught the little boy and put him on the table.

"Sing for us," he said.

"Sing for us," they all cried, forgetting about the bourgeoisie and about the Russians who make provision for the children of workmen.

The little boy began to sing in a most angelic voice. What about? Perhaps it was merely about the puppy dog he had left behind him in his village, which he would not see again until the end of the fishing season, but to me, dreaming, it seemed to be an appeal from all the children of the earth, my own child among them, to have provision made for them. And a sword of light passed before the eye of my mind, showing me that I was wrong in thinking that I could find salvation in France, where "there was a profound respect for the human intellect." For here were these Frenchmen looking for salvation to the Russians, who make provision for children.

Here, indeed, in common with all other countries, where the acquisition of wealth is the highest ambition of the individual citizen, writers are just panders to the whims of the bourgeoisie. And the bourgeoisie is a spent force, with base and lecherous whims. Its intellectual outlook has become stereotyped and stagnant, fixed in a mould. The whole structure must be uprooted and destroyed. The type must be broken up and reset in a fresh mould. "Look not for freedom to the Franks. They have a king who buys and sells." What king? The hydra-headed Bourse. The wave that flowed out over Europe from the fall of the Bastille has now spent itself. Another and more powerful wave is gushing from the oil-wells of Baku and the air is shocked by electricity from Russia's harnessed water-spouts. Long live chaos! "To't, luxury, pell-mell," for the anger of the timid must be roused by a spectacle of appalling anarchy.

We clinked our glasses and drank, not to the captain's king, but to the god of labour and peace and to the god of song, the angelic singing of children, freed from hunger and savage war. Why die while there remains this song to sing, a hymn of insurrection to the toiling masses of the world?

While we sang and drank together, I brooded on this hymn of insurrection, a tale of famine amidst plenty. The fields of golden corn are rotting in the sun, while men and women starve for want of bread. Store-rooms are packed with wool and cotton cloth, while paupers shudder in their scanty rags. Churches raised in honour of the all-loving Christ are used to shelter the homeless, while streets of houses stand empty. There lies the inspiration to write an epic of our times; no senseless "cleverness," but by writing in blood to stir the bowels of human compassion. Let the angelic voice of this child keep ringing in my ears. Then an all-consuming love will counter-act the wailing of despair and the temptations of the flesh, which keep calling on cowards to desist from the struggle.

Ho! Here is liberation. This is a fine light that pierces the thickest fog. A few years ago at Nice, when D. H. Lawrence wanted to produce a satiric paper called *The Red Rag* in conjunction with P. R. Stephenson, the latter wrote to Aldous Huxley asking his support for the idea. Huxley sent a letter saying that there was no hope for the European intellectual, that he was being overwhelmed by the ignorance of the bourgeoisie, which according to him comprised, ideologically, the toiling masses as well as the capitalists. P. R. Stephenson and myself met in a Brasserie at Nice, where we dined and drank large flagons of beer and heartily cursed the fecklessness of the arid high-brows, who are so " clever " that they see no sense in concerning themselves with " the wretched business of living."

Indeed, at supper one evening at the Café de la Paix in Paris, with Joyce, Stephens and Sullivan, the singer, Stephens said to me with emphasis that one should leave the business of living to one's valet. Rabbits! A writer must be first of all a citizen. He must be either a fellow to be expelled, crucified, or burnt in boiling oil; or else met with banners and trumpets at the outskirts of the cities which he visits. He is either an isolated voice singing in a garret, or a prophet to whom all hands are raised in homage and to whom all tongues cry out: " Hail, Christ! Hail, Mahomet! Hail, Lenin! Hail, truth and wisdom!"

One rigs one's sails according to the wind. They who

say that Shakespeare wrote for the gallery, or to tickle the palates of the groundlings, are fools. He wrote in praise of the strongest driving force of his times. And the strongest driving force of our times is the driving force of the revolutionary proletariat. That driving force is in these fishermen who sail the seas in search of tunny fish, or carry cargoes of stuff to Leningrad in the Soviet Union. They are of my kidney; not hacks, but fast-footed thoroughbreds, from the stable of Steel and Dynamo. If the intellectuals are doomed, then let us cry: "Death to the intellectuals!" Let the rich wine of revolt stir our blood to the final conflict that shall usher into the vision of man fresh conflicts about which he has not yet dreamt. Let it usher in the stars and the banners that are to be planted on the stars; the race for colonies on Mars and Jupiter, who were gods but yesterday, but which are to-day fresh territories to be trodden by human feet. Heave ho, valiant sailormen, whose naked toes find perch-holds in the wall and let the rabbit scream his bowels out in cowardly fear. We are hawks on high.

Drink up, you rowdy topers, whom have I here? A man with ruddy face, salt-mouthed, with the sea in his eyes? Go with you? Anywhere you like. No kit. Go as I am. To your island. An islander to his island. I'll go to hell and bayonet the devil. Let us go now. Give us bread and sausage. To sea. We'll put to sea and drown, or swim to heaven on a dolphin. We'll harness sharks. Let's get to hell out of here. "Thou hast lain too long by the marsh." Too true, my jolly hag. Give me a loaf. I'll vomit sin and stuff my belly full of purity. If I am to sing of famine, I must starve the glutton of my passions. I'll walk on water. I'll make a fig at death.

All together now: "*C'est le combat finale.* . . ."

## XII

WHERE was I going? Never mind. It is always good for a writer to be ready to go anywhere, with anybody, at any time. It is especially good for a writer who is contemplating suicide. Monotony, boredom and staleness lead to suicide. To set forth, no matter how, where, or with whom, is the best antidote to these evils. Therefore, when the stalwart fellows with whom I was drinking took me by the hands and asked me to accompany them, I agreed with enthusiasm. I admit that I was drunk, but at the same time I felt that I was doing the right thing.

Madame Eveno took me aside and whispered:

"But you'll be eaten with lice on that island. You'll have nothing to eat."

"I'll eat the lice," I replied.

The good woman waved her arms in despair, but my new comrades patted me on the back and said:

"There's plenty of food in the sea. We'll fish for it."

"Righto," I said. "We'll fish for it."

They were two brothers and their names were Pierre and Jean. Pierre lived on the island to which we were going and Jean was spending his holiday there with his brother. That was all I knew about them when we set forth, but it did not matter. Pierre was a splendid-looking man of thirty or so, with very powerful chest and shoulders, lean flanks and a swinging gait, which suited remarkably well his open countenance and sea-blue eyes. He looked the kind of fellow you would choose at once for a position that demanded courage and fidelity. His brother, who worked in a factory in Paris, was rather fleshy, but quite as powerfully built as Pierre. He was short in the neck and dogged-looking, like a heavy-weight boxer.

Having left the café, we staggered along the quay, carrying various packages, which the brothers were taking to their boat. Pierre had a large tin of petrol. Jean had a great sack on his back and I had a hamper of bread. We found the boat tied to the digue, got aboard the craft and put to sea at once. Even though they had drunk quite a lot, the two brothers were as active as a pair of cats once they had got their feet on the boat's timber. I sat in the stern beside Pierre, who took the tiller. Jean got the motor under way and began to rig up a mast as soon as we passed the corner of the digue, headed for the open sea. A fresh breeze came up to meet us and the boat began to roll. When the sail was set we began to ship some spray and we were soon wet to the skin. Pierre tried to make me put on an old oilskin coat that he fished out from a locker, but I laughingly refused. I wished to get drenched with brine. We all grinned at one another and felt very happy.

"This is how to live," I thought. "To drink and sing and then suddenly rush out on to the sea in a boat and feel the brine slashing against one's skin, to feel the breeze in one's nostrils and against one's teeth. To grin at one's comrades and be silent."

Even thinking was different. Now the body lived joyously and the mind was at rest; or rather active like the mind of a dog, which dreams of the chase and whines with pleasure. It dreams of its leaping body and with bared fangs lopes at the haunches of its prey. There is no questioning and victory is always to the hunter. A naked hunter brandishing his spear at dawn in a mountain glade. It was thus on a wild December day that we left Hamburg after a week in port. During the week we had all drunk heavily. My mate and I had gone without sleep for forty-eight hours. When we came aboard we had to go on watch, to get up steam and take the ship out of port. In port, a great heap of ashes had accumulated on deck, and during the last hour of the watch the engineer sent me up to throw the stuff over the side. After three hours in the stokehold, sweat was running in streams down my body. My trousers clung to my legs like a rubber glove. I was naked to the waist. The air was icy cold and a fierce wind of the North Sea screamed over the ship. Ice-cold spray came in showers over the side and beat down on my back as I shovelled the ashes into the sea. Yet I rejoiced and felt purified. Again off the African coast on another ship we ran into a heavy gale and our craft was like to founder. I was sent aft on a message by the skipper, and when I was returning to the bridge, a huge wave came towering over the ship. I clambered on to the platform of the after-mast, where I took a turn round my body with an end of rope. There I had to stay for ten minutes or so, while wave after wave poured an avalanche of wild water over the floundering ship. I shouted in ecstasy as each wave engulfed me, and during the moments that I had to hold my breath under water I felt the sweet happiness of puny man defying the most mighty of the elements. How pleased I was when the skipper caught me by the chest in his big hand, shook me like a rat and cried in his Scotch brogue: "Eh, laddie, we'll make a sailor o' ye yet."

Not on his life. Not so long afterwards, I was in Dublin, brooding over fabulous crises of the imagination. I imagined myself ill and had a morbid horror of meeting anybody I knew. I was without money and yet I could not force myself to the post-office to draw my army pension. Nor would I go home. I felt an urgent necessity to hide. I had a room in a narrow street off the North Wall, over a workmen's dining-rooms. For two days I stayed in this room without stirring out into the open air, afraid that I might meet somebody who knew me, just going downstairs for some bread and tea, when the woman came in the morning to make the bed. Then I would hurry back into the room and sit on the bed, staring at the floor. I would not wash as there was a dead spider in the wash-basin beside the water-jug. It had been drowned spreading its web in the basin. It was I myself drowned it the first morning, when I went to empty some water from the jug into the basin. Seeing the insect trying to escape from the water, I had put down the jug and drawn back. It was overwhelmed and drowned by the sudden splash caused by the jug being dropped into the water I had poured. And there it remained. Sometimes I would rise from the bed and walk slowly across the room to the wash-stand in order to look at the insect's carcass. And it grew increasingly horrible, until at last I had to get up and leave the room in the middle of the night. I walked about the quays until daybreak, and then, when the sun rose, my black mood went away, leaving me amazed at my recent conduct. I felt violently hungry and set off towards the post-office where I could draw my pension. I hung about that street until the post-office opened, and when the official gave me the money, I went away gloriously happy.

"What is the meaning of this? Why should I rejoice when the waves came pouring over my head and I was in danger of being swept overboard to a certain death, or be indifferent to the freezing cold of the North Sea, stripped to the waist, and yet cower in a room for two days in mortal terror of a drowned spider? Why am I now happy, going off to a strange island with strangers, just a few hours after wanting to commit suicide?"

I smiled at these questions, for I really was not interested in them. I slipped off my shoe and put my bare foot over the side of the boat into the water.

"Don't do that," said Pierre. "There are sharks about here. You might lose your foot."

I laughed and pulled back my foot, and then I wondered what he would say if I told him about the dead spider. He would undoubtedly think that I was mad; especially if I told him that my horror of the spider and my staying in that room alone for two days was a manifestation of a mania for "going into hiding" which has beset me since the war. Then, of course, he would change his mind about taking me to his island. He would race his boat back to Concarneau and get rid of me.

Being still under the influence of the wine I had drunk

and probably also suffering from the effect of the morning's nervous crisis, I found a malicious pleasure in the deception I was playing on the worthy fellow. Then I reflected with great interest how I had from my earliest youth suffered occasionally from the mania for "going into hiding." So it was not due to the war, although the war intensified it. Even as a little boy, in the midst of a daydream, when I caught somebody looking at me, or perhaps it was the schoolmaster in the village school who shouted at me to wake up and attend to my work, I had a strong inclination to run away and hide. Why? Because I was sure they would kill me, the people, if they found out what I was thinking about. They would say: "He has the inner sight. He is sold to the devil. Let us kill him." Why that should be so, it is difficult to explain, but it is undoubtedly a mania from which I have suffered ever since the creative urge came to life in me. But then, what is that creative urge other than a form of insanity, an overbalancing of the physical organism; more likely due to some "lack" in the organism than to the presence of some quality not possessed by the ordinary male. To females I deny this creative urge, except in so far as they feel the urge to create children. And that urge in itself is the outcome of a "lack" in their construction.

The sea around the boat became a living thing to me as I brooded on this strange thought, while I chatted to Pierre about his life on the island. The sea's surface was unbroken, but it rolled in heavy waves. It made no sound except where it swirled against the boat's sides and chugged against its bow now and again. This silence of the moving mass of water beneath the screaming wind made me feel that the sea was a great kind god carrying me to his palace, while the wind was a hostile demon trying to prevent my escape. What friendly power was in the sleek sides of the green waves! What affection in their caress of the boat's sides! What great wisdom in their mysterious silence, stretching away on either side to the horizon!

Hurrah! Once more I breast the wall defiantly. My arrogant soul has forgotten defeat and the sour hatred of defeat. The little sorceress has kindled a fire within my navel. She has hung up her pot and fanned the licking flames with her skirt. The words bubble in the pot. Let's look into it. A fine brew. Shall I take this radiant bubble in my pipe and suck God's beauty from it? What a gorgeous feast! Now horror is transformed to the noble blood-lust of the conqueror and in the sunny spray my soul is scoured of its tarnish. Can it be true that a few hours ago I looked at a garden all in bloom and only saw corruption? That I had less courage than a tiny insect which defends its life with the last particle of its energy? For shame.

Once upon a beach in Donegal I watched a sand insect build its lair. In order to annoy it, I put a pebble against the door it had made. At once it came out and with great labour cleared away the pebble. Then it retired into its hole. Again I put the pebble there, choking up the doorway. Once more it came forth and laboured savagely until it had removed the obstruction. For half an hour I kept putting up the pebble and the insect kept taking it away, until at last it was exhausted and could not remove the pebble properly. Then I had pity on it and felt so impressed by its courage and perseverance that I would have spent the rest of the day seeking it a supply of food for the winter had I but known what it ate.

Truly, one must dare everything, since it may be in the foulest mire that one may find the most precious jewel. If I have been a tavern sot and "made myself a motley to the view," I have the descent of Christ into hell for a precedent. *De profundis clamavi at te dominum.* The greatest virtue of genius is permanent dissatisfaction. While the fire burns beneath the pot of the sorceress, the throbbing motor of the heart drives on the soul to conquest. Neither by the marsh nor on the mountain can it rest, for the highest peak merely serves the eye as a vantage-point from which to see a higher peak, across a more dangerous defile than any hitherto encountered. And there is no heaven other than the joy of the ascent. Between two mountains is always the pit, floored with mire, in darkness, peopled with babbling ghouls, while about the edge the black-cowled monks of mediocrity snarl their hatred of the struggling poet. Not a hand is stretched out to help. "He thought himself god, did he? Now is our chance to strike him while he is down. Later, when he scales the height once more, radiant in a greater splendour, our sins shall put us to a greater shame."

Suddenly the wind died down completely. The movement of the sea became more languid. The sail flapped idly on the mast. A group of little islands stood out clearly against the horizon ahead of us. A mass of dun clouds, streaked with red by the sunlight, lay beyond the islands, and above the clouds the sky was a spotless blue. The sea was dotted with fishing boats and away to starboard there was a large ship, with a column of smoke from her funnels, bearing down on us. Pierre told his brother to abandon the sail. Jean unwillingly did so.

Pierre laughed and said to me:

"He prefers to sail a boat, but I prefer the motor. I like to feel the power of the motor driving the boat. But Jean works all the year in Paris, so he prefers the sail. It's because it's so different from the life of Paris, where he hears motors all day every day in his factory."

"How strange it is," I thought, "that I should be here with these men whom I do not know, going to their island for an unknown purpose. But is it really an accident, or was I destined to meet them and to go with them?"

Jean sat down after having put away the mast and the sail. We lit cigarettes.

"I am forty-two," he said. "In my early days at sea it was all sail. When I served my time in the navy even, I did more sailing than under steam. Were you in the war?"

"Yes," I said. "I was in the war."

"During the war," he said, "I served on land, in the marine division. Do you see that?"

He pulled up his trousers off his right leg and showed the scars of a huge wound that had mangled the limb from the knee almost to the ankle.

"That must have been a bad one," I said.

"You are right," he answered. "It was terrible. I lay on my belly for ten hours with that wound, fighting the whole time. Sometimes I propped myself up against the side of the hole and fought the bastards with my bayonet when they attacked. We did not let them pass. We were all sailors, who knew little about fighting on land, in trenches, but we held our position and kept back forty thousand Germans with a few thousand Breton sailors. That was at the beginning of the war on the Belgian coast. Only a handful of us came back. From all this Breton coast thousands of fine men went north, but only a few came south again. They lie up there. We held the Germans back all the same, forty thousand of them. And now they come again, the bastards."

"It's not their fault, Jean," said Pierre. "They are driven to the slaughter just the same as we are, or the English, or the soldiers of any other bourgeois country."

"I know that," said Jean. "I wasn't referring to the German workers, but to the Nazi Germans. However, it's hard to see the difference between one German and another, whether he calls himself a Communist or a Fascist. They are always ready to follow anybody who puts uniforms on them and leads them to the slaughter. They were always that way. They are a barbarous and uncivilized race. I think it's a great pity they did not occupy France in 1870 with their whole army and stay there. Then they would all have gone to bed with French women and eaten properly and they'd be a civilized people by now."

"It's that sort of talk that keeps the working class of the world where it is," said Pierre.

"Still, there is some sense in it," I said.

I just wanted to keep them arguing, so that I could be silent myself. What interest could I have any longer in the rival virtues of the Germans and the French? Or whether workmen are driven to slaughter one another by Fascist chiefs or Communist commisars? It's the movement that counts, provided there is movement. It is better for the poet to find the life surrounding him dangerous and difficult than to find it safe and easy. When it is safe and easy, the poet fiddles with Nero the fiddler, while the Rome of his imagination rots. No matter what we may say of war, we who deplore its horror and its pain, we must admit that it is the greatest inspiration of the poet. It has been, you say, but not in the future. But who can read the future, except God, whom we have not yet perfected? We can no more read the future than the priest, who claimed to be a prophet, could give the next day's three o'clock winner to Charles II at Newmarket. "Give us the winner of the three o'clock," said the king, "and I'll believe you are a prophet." The priest gave him a stumor.

When the fire is out, when I wallow in the mire of the pit between two heights, I can take sides with the Germans against the French, or with the Communists against the Fascists, or with Zoroaster against Buddha; because then it is necessary to take sides and to have a patron. But when the little sorceress fans the flames within my navel and I am on the height, human controversy about right and wrong is like the anarchic screeching of the wind above the overwhelming sea. Then all is holy. What difference does it make whether he got that horrid wound in heroic battle with his country's foes, defending fair vineyards and the sweet breasts of his dote from the plundering Huns, or in a stinking brothel, hocked by a pimp's knife? The difference lies in the telling of it.

"Look at that swine," Pierre cried suddenly. "Look at that floating prison."

He pointed to the ship that was bearing down on us. It was a French light cruiser on her way to Brest. She was passing close to us and we could see men standing on her decks. We could see her sheathed guns and all her death-dealing tackle, sinister in their grey paint. I noticed that Jean and Pierre lowered their voices when cursing her, as if they were afraid that she might hear, turn on them and ram them to the bottom of the sea with her slim prow. To them she was a monster. When she passed they raised their voices again and railed against the bourgeoisie, which spends the money stolen from fishermen to build these floating prisons, where the sons of fishermen are trained to act as the jailers and oppressors of their kindred, should the latter try to free themselves from the chains of slavery.

"Nearly all the fishermen on this coast are Socialists," Pierre said. "One day I was fishing here and I saw a sardine boat with a red sail on which the owner had painted a sickle and hammer. A cruiser passed just like that one and the man stood up in the stern and shook his fist at her and cursed. It was queer because he had a wooden leg, instead of the leg he had lost in the war. There he was standing on his wooden leg beside his red sail with the sickle and hammer of Bolshevism on it, cursing the cruiser. If they had any sense they'd know what's coming to them. But they'll go on persecuting us until the day comes when their guts are ripped open and they're dumped over the side. It will happen in every navy in the world. Men who go to sea have more guts than men in factories. They'll be the first to rise."

I felt thrilled by his enthusiasm and by the determination in his calm voice. Here was no foul scavenger of cigarette ends, skulking around the door of Notre-Dame cathedral, but a strong and brave young man, hardened by constant labour on the dangerous sea. I had no doubt that he would rip open bowels and hook out hearts with his jack knife if he so felt inclined. He looked a leader of men, sober in judgment, polite in manner and of such stability that he could leap from a bout of heavy drinking to steer his boat in a gale. It is by such men that revolutions are made, and if there are many such men in western Europe then there is no danger for the future of our civilization.

Here is truth, then, and virtue and God and certainty; to be at one with men like Pierre, who are going to be the aristocrats of the future. Men who worship machines and shall be masters of machines and shall use them for the welfare of mankind. Not aristocrats who sit on money-bags and dine on prunes and biscuits, who buy women and do the glutton in their yachts, who hire nations to fight in order to sell their armaments and send millions to their death in unflowered youth. No, but here is the restoration of true aristocracy, about which a poet may sing an epic without being a pander. The rule of men who regard the giving of service as the highest virtue, men chosen for leadership for their manliness, their wisdom and their generosity.

Come, bald scholars, off with your skull-caps and your

dressing-gowns. Burn your anthologies of dead men's verses and listen to the song that's on the wind. Throw away your pansies, slim æsthetes, and carry the wild rose of insurrection. "Every man to his post." And let the women as well turn away from the tepid water of sex-weariness to fill their starved wombs with fruitful seed. Damn your stinking wells and your dull tales of last year's fornications. Come, sing us a wild song of revolt.

Look! The sea-hags, perched on their dirt-caked rock, bob their long necks uneasily at our approach and dive into the sea. Away filth! We are purified.

### XIII

It was coming on towards sunset when we pulled in at the little jetty on our island, after passing a number of fishing boats and small yachts riding at anchor. I was rather disappointed at finding yachts in the place, but Pierre assured me that the occupants did not come ashore. They merely sheltered there for the night. A small boy paddled out to meet us in a punt as we came near the jetty and he cried out something in Breton. In answer to his question, Pierre took a small package from his pocket and tossed it into the punt. The little boy pounced on the package, glanced at me shyly and then paddled back furiously to the jetty. I noticed that, in spite of his obvious delight at getting the package, whatever it was, he made no immediate attempt to examine its contents. Instead, he helped to make fast the boat, just like a grown up person. This impressed me very much and made me feel very pleased. Obviously it was an island on which there were no loafers and where the struggle of life gave a manly dignity and a noble silence even to children.

It looked strange and even forbidding at first sight. There was a huge square vat for storing lobsters and crayfish above the jetty, and on the near wall of this immense vat were hung the heads of tunny fish in clusters. It reminded me of the heads that were hung on the gates of feudal mansions; heads of slaughtered enemies. When I stepped ashore, I found the ground strewn with great quantities of shells and fish offal. And then I became aware that there was a menacing silence in the place. It was unlike the silence of the sea, which was a silence of movement, suggesting strength and certainty of achievement, an unchangeableness that imparts courage to one who is carried along its back. This silence was like the silence of a graveyard, or of a monastery where men meditate on death. Although it was sunset there were no birds singing; nor indeed did there seem to be any birds, except the solemn cormorants and seagulls which stood on the outlying rocks. Although there were a number of men about the place they hardly made a sound, talking in low whispers, or shuffling along slowly over the shells in heavy wooden clogs.

And in obedience to this solemnity, I became silent within myself; expectant like one waiting for a strange manifestation of nature; an eclipse of the sun, or the appearance of a monster in the sky, a god-monster of the Apocalypse. I walked up the jetty, past a group of men who sat against the side of a ruined boat. They barely answered my salutation and did not even look after me when I had passed. There were two houses on my right, and the space between them, they faced one another, was strewn with a great quantity of refuse, principally fish offal. It was just as if the human beings had adapted themselves to the habits of sea-birds and left things which they no longer needed exactly where they dropped them as useless. In fact, while I paused to look, I was startled by a woman's arm appearing through a window of the house more remote from the jetty, to hurl the fresh-peeled skin of a rabbit on to the other refuse. I shuddered and turned away.

"You'll be eaten by lice," Madame Eveno had said.

I began to be really afraid of the place and wondered what devil had inspired me to come to it. Had I been driven here by my impulse towards self-destruction? This thought made me see clearly in my mind that that impulse was artificial, for I trembled lest I might be in the power of a demon stronger than my will to live and that I had come here to be destroyed by him. This dreadful, menacing silence!

I walked past a life-boat house and a great water tank built into the earth. Then I stood on the summit of the island. Not a tree except a solitary fig tree, stunted and bedraggled, standing at the gable of a small house, in a hollow about three hundred yards away. The island was a heap of rock and sand, which was covered with sparse, rough grass of a faded colour. In this light the grass looked dark brown, for the mists of evening had already settled on it. It seemed to run before the eyes, like all things which have no particular colour or character. Truly, it was as dreary as a churchyard. In the distance, at the far end of the island, there were thin columns of smoke rising from pits where men were burning seaweed for kelp. I could see the figures of the kelp burners against the horizon, lifting up strands of dried seaweed and spreading them over the burning pits. Their movements were slow and suggestive of despair. I could feel the expression on their faces; the solemn stare of those who gaze at infinity and find it awesome.

The air was pungent with the smell of the burning seaweed and then there was the biting smell of the sea coming up on the wind. I walked ahead towards the other side of the island. Lizards hopped from the path and then I stood still, having seen a rat stare at me. It stood by a little heap of stones that were almost covered with briars. It stared at me with its half blind eyes and then slowly moved away, so fat that it could hardly move. It struggled down into a crevice between two stones and I could see its brown body panting there. Dying?

Another hundred yards and I was at the far side of the island. What a contrast to the filth of the side where I had landed. A beautiful sandy beach stretched for hundreds of yards on either side of me. It was bare except for one large sea plant left there by the receding tide. The plant was still wet with brine and it shone in the light of the sunset. It looked so beautiful after the rabbit skin that had been thrown out the window. It was about eight feet long, tapering to a point and lined on both sides with a series of intricate frills, just like a scarf of a sea princess. I strode down on to the beach to feast my eyes on its beauty more closely; but as soon as I stepped on the sand, which had appeared so pure and uninhabited from the bank above, I dislodged a vast horde of insects from my path. They filled the air as thick as locusts, flew a little way and then dropped again on the sand, where they deftly buried themselves. On the sea-plant itself there was a great multitude of them, which flew into the air when I raised up its end. I dropped it in disgust and ground my teeth. Corruption everywhere!

I strode quickly to the left, where there were pebbles on the beach and a strip of rock left naked by the ebbing tide. I jumped on to the rock and stamped the sand from my shoes. Let me have cleanliness or I shall go mad. I stood still and looked about me, listening. I saw green flies hopping about and I heard the crunching of the crabs crawling on the rocks beneath the yellow weeds. What? This sound that cheered me but a few days ago, reminding me of home and childhood and famished appetite, now brought before my mind a picture of disgusting slime and worms that feed on corruption.

"Then does nothing exist outside the mind? Or has a devil truly entered into me, making foul what is most fair? Has he fixed a mirror of pollution to my eyes and warped my senses, so that I can only absorb impressions that plant daggers in my wounded reason?"

My eyes dilated and I looked about me like a tortured beast which has taken refuge in a dark cave from his enemies and sees imaginary eyes watching him; the eyes of his pursuers projected by his fear. And then a voice shouted:

"So you thought you had got away with it, eh?"

I looked behind me, but there was nobody. Then I shuddered and bowed my head. And the voice said again:

"Now I'm going to be kind to you, as I think you have suffered enough. At least you might suffer so much as to be of no further use to me. You might die, or break down completely, and in either case you would spoil my purpose. The dreadful thing is that one is given only one body. I'll get you someone to look after you, since you can't look after yourself and do my work at the same time. It would be better if I could make you young again instead of having to deal with another person as well as you."

"But was I ever young?" I cried.

"Not in the ordinary sense," he said, "but you were better capable of reproducing in my work the ecstasy of youth. You have lost that."

"Have I, indeed? Just now when I was in the boat . . ."

"That is all nonsense. Just now in the boat you got excited about social revolution. That is a form of idealism that would be absolutely ruinous to my work if I allowed you to become really infected by it. You might as well put on a soutane and read a breviary and say Mass. If a writer makes himself the idol of the mob by voicing the ambitions of the mob, then he is reduced to the common level of the mob's intelligence. The mob will not allow him to rise above that level. A writer . . ."

"But I don't want to rise above the level of the mob, as you call the mass of my fellow-men."

"You'll have to do so or die. I'd really kill you if you became a mob worshipper. But of course you couldn't. You are merely a coward, prepared to attach yourself to anybody when danger threatens."

"Christ! How hopeless it all is! One moment I am convinced that I have rehabilitated myself and at the next I am cast down into a deeper pit than ever."

"That is not so. You have escaped, but you don't realize it. The pit is not this torture of the mind from which you now suffer, a continual vacillation between one enthusiasm and another, a rapid passage from despair to exaltation and from exaltation to despair. It is indifference. It is the indifference born of a continual satisfaction of the passions, or worse still, of a self-satisfaction that quenches the fire in the soul. Here is the earth in all its nakedness, without flowers or trees or birds to make it tame and friendly. There is the sea, sombre and dangerous in the light of evening. There is the air, grown cold, to give you an indication of the storms that buffet man. But all that is good if you accept it as good. If you fear it and turn aside from it to hide in the artificial sewers of cities, that means you have lost contact with life, that it has become an alien. The earth, the sea and the air are man's substance and his sustenance. What man builds on earth and his contraptions for mastering the elements are ephemeral and alien to nature. Renew your friendship with nature. In that lies your chance of regaining peace."

The voice had fallen from a shout to a gentle whisper and then it drifted into a puff of wind that blew about my face. My fear departed and I became cunning as I climbed the sand-bank going towards the houses.

"I have arrived here, in any case," I said to myself, " and even though it looks a dreadful place I must make the best of it."

At the gable end of the lifeboat house I came across two hens that had salvaged some fish offal and were devouring the beastly morsel greedily. They were the most frightful pair of hens that I had ever seen. Their feathers were all askew. They had hardly any flesh on their bones and one of them had her head turned sideways, as the result of some disease. Probably malnutrition. I passed them with my head turned away in disgust. Between the lifeboat house and the dwelling-house I saw a gate opened into a yard that was covered with dung and refuse. A girl was milking a cow within the gate. While she was being milked the cow was gnawing at an empty sardine tin. Like the hens, she was all skin and bone. Her reddish coat was faded and she gazed at me in a frightened way for a few moments. Then she tossed her battered horns and continued to gnaw at the sardine tin.

When I reached the front of the house I heard angry voices arguing. It was Pierre talking to his wife.

"Ha!" I thought. "She is barging him for having brought me to the island. This is a nice kettle of fish."

However, it was now too late to get away. There would be no means of getting back to the mainland, unless I got a lift from one of the yachts in the harbour. In any case I would have to stay the night. But why go? Would it not be better to make friends with the woman?

Unless I could persuade these islanders to accept me, there seemed no great sense in going on with the business of living. And now I wanted to live very much. All the poverty and hunger that surrounded me made me love life, just as the immense wealth of London had made me disgusted with life. So I drew back my shoulders and turned in at the first door I reached. It led into a long passage where it was already quite dark. To the left of this passage I found a bar in which a number of fishermen were drinking. Although it was not yet dark outside, a lamp was lit in the bar and I could barely distinguish the faces of the drinkers. The lamp stood on a shelf behind the counter, beside a wench that was serving the drinks. I noticed that she limped when she moved. It seemed that nearly every living thing on the island had some defect.

I took a seat on a form by a table and waited, but nobody took any notice of me. I understood nothing of what the men were saying as they spoke in Breton. They spoke in whispers, slowly, just like the men who were conversing outside. It seemed to me as if it were forbidden by law to talk loudly on this island.

At last I stood up and went to the counter, where I ordered a glass of red wine.

"Hell!" I said to myself. "I must make these people merry or I'll go mad."

I invited two men who were leaning against the counter to drink with me. They made no reply, but after a few moments they emptied their glasses and pushed them across the counter towards the girl who was pouring my wine from a bottle. Then they wiped their mouths on their sleeves and clasped their hands behind their backs. She filled their glasses after having filled mine. Slowly she pushed the filled glasses across the counter towards us.

"How much?" I said.

At first she bowed her head and flushed deeply. Then she looked timidly at the two fishermen and muttered the price of the drinks. I passed her a coin and she brought back the change.

"Keep it," I said.

She flushed still more deeply and limped away to the corner of the counter.

"Take it," one of the fishermen said. "He doesn't mean any harm."

But she would not come near us. She kept shrugging her shoulders and blushing in the corner, until another man entered the bar and ordered a drink.

"This is very odd," I thought.

"Why wouldn't she take the tip?" I said to the fisherman who had spoken to her.

"She is not in the habit," he said. "Among our people it is not the custom to take tips. It is only in towns and such places where strangers are in the habit of coming that tips are taken. She is a shy girl. We are a shy people, we Bretons; but we mean no evil by it."

*Sursum corda!* How beautiful to find on this wretched island, strewn with offal and crawling with lizards, rats, lice and flies that feed on corruption, such human delicacy of manner! And I reflected that it is the pursuit of gain which is most degrading to the human character. Tips, dividends and royalties. They all produce loathsome characteristics in men and women. There is the root of the evil that has brought us face to face with the idea of our civilization's downfall. Happily for us, the nature of the evil became manifest to us before the disaster was upon us. A few years ago, on my way to the Balearic Islands, I took a taxi in Barcelona from the station to the Palma boat. I offered to tip the driver at the end of the journey, but he refused with dignity, saying that the correct reward for his service was marked on the clock. I was greatly impressed by this. I apologized and bowed to him. He plucked off his cap and returned my bow with the graciousness and dignity of a nobleman. In Russia it is illegal to tip a worker for his services. In Italy the same law holds good. Very likely the Germans and the Japanese, who, in spite of their barbarous excesses in many ways, have the knack of imitating what redounds to the glory of their neighbours, are going to make similar laws in their countries. Very soon it will become universal. The worker will have regained the dignity which was his in primitive society, when as a hunter, or a shepherd, or a solitary peasant, he would disdain to accept payment for hospitality and merely exchanged goods in obedience to his personal necessities. The evil of money will have passed away.

What a liberation that will be! If one allows the imagination to dwell on the real meaning of that socialist phrase, " Production for use and not for profit," one can visualize a society composed solely of ladies and gentlemen. And for us writers that would be a greater liberation than for practically any other group in society, except perhaps those scientists who nowadays, instead of being engaged in the battle against disease and death, are forced to invent death-dealing gases and explosives and machines. When a woman sells her body either in the huckster's stall of whoredom or in the wholesale store of " marriage for money," every decent conscience is horrified by this sacrilege against the laws of nature. But few people understand that it is more sacrilegious to sin against the intellect than against the body.

" That is the problem that I have got to solve," I thought as I toasted my comrades in the fresh glass of wine, " the problem of how to live and support my family without having to depend on writing for doing so. It is really the problem I set out to solve when I left London. As long as I have to depend on my writing for money I must always be subject to these occasional fits of despair. But how can that be done? "

I looked at the faces of the two fishermen with whom I was drinking. Did they look happy? They were, as far as I knew, leading the sort of life that appears idyllic to the tired worker in the city, the man who goes into his stuffy office every day and toils at his desk, without enthusiasm, or the feeling that he is expressing himself in some vital and necessary way and then goes home at night to his wife and family in the suburbs after the sun has gone down. He dreams, perhaps, of being a fisherman or a farmer and to feel the sun on his back or the rain on his face while he works. But do these fishermen dream of working in the city, where life is gayer and where the nights are brighter than the gloomy days of their solitude on the sea or on the farm?

Certainly their faces did not seem to be those of happy

men. The tall man, Antoine, looked very haggard and sad. He was raggedly dressed and his shoulders stooped, like a man defeated in the struggle of life. His curly black hair stood out at the back of his neck, beneath the rim of his tattered white hat. Pol, the little man, looked even more melancholy. His round face was blotched and his eyes were bloodshot. They reminded one of the eyes of a sick dog. He was even more ragged than Antoine and his posture was more despondent.

I ordered a bottle of wine and asked them to sit down at the table with me. Then they began to talk freely.

"Forgive us," Pol said, "for not being able to stand our round of drink while we are drinking with you, but we have no money. Antoine and I are from the mainland. We came in here to try our luck for a few weeks, but nothing came our way except a few mullet. It is a hard life, the life of a fisherman these days. The only chance is to get a place in a tunny boat. Ah, sir, the life of a working man is a hard one."

"It is dreadful," Antoine said. "That place we all sleep in across the way is terrible with lice, and then there's no proper food. We can't afford to eat the fish we catch. There's nothing, only crabs and food out of tins. A man longs for a good stew or fish soup. A man might as well starve at home as here. We haven't earned a hundred francs during the fortnight we are here. And we relied on this trip for making enough to give us a start over the coming winter. I don't know what's going to happen to my wife and family this winter."

"Damn it!" I thought. "Why was I complaining? What a humbug I have been to think my position was pitiable when I had enough every day to fill my stomach and the stomachs of my family. That is the important thing, really the only important thing in life. To have food and shelter and health."

" Ah," said Pol, " you have a wife and family to worry about, but I have nobody. I had a wife and daughter, sir, but I lost them. Indeed, I don't care what happens to me. I go on living and I often ask myself why I go on living. I suffer hardship, but I know I would suffer just the same if I had millions. My misery is in the heart and not anywhere else. One can cure the miseries of the stomach, but it is hard to cure the miseries of the heart."

Tears came into his bloodshot eyes and he emptied his glass. I filled it again from the bottle.

" What a weathercock I am! " I thought. " No sooner have I come to the conclusion about the stomach being the vital centre of life than this man shifts my conviction towards the heart. But wait. I may learn the truth from these simple men. It was men like these who were chosen by Christ as possessors and teachers of the truth. Fishermen and little children."

" Money can do a lot," said Antoine.

" It can," I said, eager to make Pol talk.

Pol shook his head and angrily swallowed his glass once more. Tears rolled down his cheeks. He had suddenly become drunk, not so much as the result of drinking the wine as through the memory of his sorrow coming to the front of his consciousness.

" It can do nothing for a sick heart," he said. " Why do I try to make myself drunk? It's trying to kill the memory of her death. She died three years ago, sir, but the years do not help me. She was a good wife and I loved her dearly. I can't get over the thought that she's no longer there. When I wake up in the morning even yet I want to say good morning to her, and I look beside me in the bed and I suffer just as bitterly not finding her there as when I looked at her corpse for the first time. It's a terrible loneliness. The loss of my daughter is not so much. We could have had another daughter had Julia lived. But to find another Julia, that is impossible. The little Adele belonged to her, not to me. But Julia belonged to me. We were two parts of the same person, and when we were together there was great peace on the earth. I always felt it like that. When we sat down to eat together, there was no need to talk. Or walking along the road with her. We saw things in the same way, whether it was the sun shining or the rain falling. If I had a pain then she shared it, just by being there, and it was the same way when she had a pain. It was impossible in that way to be unhappy. If I had been in prison with her, even if we went together to the guillotine, it would not be hard to endure it, because there would be no loneliness. It was that way."

Antoine looked at me and said:

"I keep trying to tell him that it's no use worrying about what can't be changed, but it's no use. I keep telling him to get another wife, but he prefers thinking of her he has lost. He'll kill himself that way."

"But it's fine all the same," I thought. "The way he carries his grief always with him is purifying. I am on the track of something here. Let us wait. The heavens are opening. A rainbow?"

Pierre came into the room leading his wife by the hand. He was laughing.

"She is angry with me," he said, "because she thinks there is no proper accommodation here for you. But I told her you are a man like us. What is good for us is good for you. That's what I told her. You are a writer and we are fishermen, but you also are a worker like us. I said that to her, but she won't believe me. She said I had no right to bring you here, as there is no fit accommodation or food. Speak to her, Guillaume."

She was a thin-faced, shy little woman, but my heart went out to her at once. There was such delicacy and modesty in her carriage and in her eyes. I got up, took her hand, kissed it and said that in the village where I was born the accommodation was poorer than on her island, but that the hearts of the people there were gentle as here, and that we had a proverb which said a dry potato from a generous heart was better than a rich feast without love.

"We are fisher folk too," I said. "Although I speak a different language, we are of the same race. Please treat me as a neighbour."

"We are of the same race because we are workers," Pierre cried. "That is the important thing."

"God made us all," Antoine said.

"God is here," cried Pierre, striking his great chest.

"And here," he cried, bending up his magnificent biceps.

"And here," he cried, tapping his forehead. "The priests tell us only about devils that need money. Give me a glass, Guillaume, and I'll drink with you. Sit down, sweetheart, and drink with us."

He put his arm around his wife's waist and took her on his knee. She struggled shyly to get away from him, but there was no escape from that powerful grip. Pol snivelled, very likely thinking of the time he last took his Julia on his knee. But Pierre hit him a whack between the shoulder-blades and said something to him, laughingly, in Breton. The melancholy Pol laughed with the others. Then everybody got very happy. Jean soon joined us with a large plate of crabs, which we began to eat. With the loaf I had taken with me in the boat, an enormous loaf used by tunny fishermen, and the wine and the delicious crabs, we made a hearty meal. Everybody was happy. We all talked at the top of our voices. We drank several bottles of wine. The limping maid brought us coffee and sat down to table with us. Then I offered the company some liqueurs. The maid got up, stood against the wall and sang a melancholy song, like the ones I used to hear at home. I felt near to tears with a sad, gentle sort of happiness.

And when I mounted to my bed and lay down and listened to the murmur of the sea through the open window I felt that peace beyond understanding, which infects the soul as the result of perfect communion with other souls. There was no furniture in the room except the rude bed and a washstand that was still more rude. Only the protection of the walls and the bed-covering made my lot different from that of the wild birds on their rocks and the lizards crouching in the withered grass. Mysterious night was so near me that I could feel it like a substance. So that I felt timid and yet I was glad to feel timid, for it was the timidity which makes man pray to his God. "Lord! Lord! Protect me, for I am afraid."

Which God, indeed? Which prophet is the true one? Men may lie as they will, but unless they can humiliate themselves and bow down before the God of love, their life is barren of true happiness. That is the real meaning of the saying: "What does it benefit a man if he gains the whole world and suffers the loss of his own soul?" We have grown so tired of priestly cant and hypocrisy that we have turned against the wisdom which their avarice had corrupted by use as a cover for their evil-doing; but we must return to its simple beauty if we wish to save ourselves. There is more loveliness in the embrace of a little child than in the victories of Alexander, or in the barren calculations of the greatest scientist.

How strange it is that we have grown ashamed of love! And most ashamed of the love that is loveliest, of suffering little children to come unto us, of being like them!

Death is now a monster.

## XIV

HERE I am just risen from my bed, trying to recapture my emotions on arising from my bed on that island off the Breton coast. If I cannot recapture them, I cannot write the truth. How difficult it is! The road is up somewhere and the band of my old regiment is marching down Ebury Street with the new guard. How fine that is! The pipers in their beautiful saffron uniforms look to me much finer than the pipers of the Scots Guards. But I come away from the window, fold my arms and force my mind back to Brittany and to the thoughts that struck me on arising that other morning. It's no longer the same. I sit down and pick up the newspapers, in order to escape from reality by glancing over their fantastic contents.

"General Goemboes, the Hungarian premier, has hurriedly left Budapest for Vienna." Why has he gone to Vienna? The newspaper toys for a little while with reasons for his visit and then goes on to say: "The odds are two to one on Petersen in his fight with Harvey." I decide to support Harvey, because I lost money on the victory of Petersen over Doyle. I study Petersen's superiority in weight and reach. I get jealous of his chances and turn over to the racing page. There I am intrigued by the following item: "Given a moderate run of luck over the winter months, one cannot but feel convinced that Kilcash Hill is going to be concerned with the finish of the Grand National. So far, the danger to this promising performer over the major obstacles seems to be the consistent Alpine Hut." I flatter myself by thinking that I am more shrewd than the newswriter, by saying to myself that I will give another chance to Heartbreak Hill and then I turn to the leader page, where I read the following: "Now that the old year is drawing to a close and unseasonal weather has forced us towards brooding on the problems of the new year, we must admit that the major problem of 1934 is the selection of England's leading pair against Australia. Sutcliffe is an automatic choice, but the question of the most suitable partner for this great batsman is a very open one."

Before my mind can really concern itself with this major problem of the new year, I find that the Poles can turn out a complete outfit of clothes for seven and sixpence. And then I am astounded by the following item of news. "After Amar Nath had knocked up his century yesterday, he was mobbed by rich Hindu women, who took off their ornaments, diamond rings from their noses, fingers and ears, as well as bracelets and anklets, offering them to Amar Nath with the reverence due to a god. Hindu millionaires also presented the batsman with cheques. A Moslem millionaire gave him a cheque for £750. Other gifts included two gold cups, a dozen gold medals, silver and gold images, gold watches and a motor-car. Several coolies were required to take the presents away."

Here I hope to find cause for irritation with the injustice of bourgeois society, which gives such prominence and fantastic rewards to people and animals that hit one another, or hit balls with bats, or jump over fences. I rush to my writing-desk with the intention of composing a tirade against the insult to human intelligence implied in that sentence, "several coolies were required to take the presents away," while no mention is made of the number of men and women who spent the cold winter's night on the seats in the parks and on the embankments.

But before I can begin, I remember Edward Garnett saying to me: "To the artist, everything that exists justifies itself by the fact of its existence." What a scoundrel, therefore, the artist must be! A much greater hypocrite and scoundrel, judging him from a humanitarian point of view, than the financier, in his city lair, filching the savings of the widow and the orphan with fair promises of gold from mines in Utopia. For I might sing of Amar Nath, or denounce him, just as I might sing of the injustice of letting people perish in the wintry cold for lack of houses; but I could not sing at all if there were nothing to sing about.

And indeed, that helps me to recapture my emotions on awaking at dawn on the Breton island. I had rushed forth into the open air, to draw into my lungs the exuberance of the morning and to do the simple chores of an animal, indifferent to care. During my sleep, my vitality had been renewed, and if I had thought, at that moment, of Goemboes's voyage, of Petersen's purse, or of Amar Nath's treasures, I would have smiled in pleasure at the glorious and varied manifestations of human activity on this planet. No rancour would stir my soul by the contemplation of injustice. There, in the dawn, on a wild island, nothing unpleasant impinged on my consciousness, for I was lord of all I surveyed. There was no rent to pay, nor foul linen to be sent to the laundry, nor publishers to telephone for their script. There I was, if not *primus inter pares* like a king, at least *liber inter pares*, like a citizen of a civilized society, which I hope some day to see on the road to its accomplishment.

Is that the truth I set out to find? To take joy in movement and to bear sorrow gladly, knowing that in its endurance I find words for my songs. Would it were the truth.

But there stands the spectre of famine and bestial war

that follows in its trail and all the manifold cruelties that give the lie to the ambitious motto on man's coat of arms: "One day I shall be God." Artist, or thief, or cricketer, or vagrant wretch, I have the common and universal duty to fulfil, that I must help towards the liberation of the human intellect from the spectre of famine. That is the truth. Not the truth for all times, while there are men on earth. Such a truth, perhaps, cannot be found. Sufficient for the day and generation is the truth thereof.

And yet, I swear that I was happier that morning than I am now, for I was indifferent to truth, or to my duty as a human being to mourn the plight of my suffering brothers and sisters. I went forth and saw the birds wheeling in the air, or hopping about the rocks, or diving into the sea for fish. Each one, to my glance, seemed free among its equals, and its freedom was sufficient to me. They gladdened my eyes and my mind did not ponder on their ceaseless toil from morning to night in search of food, how they are a prey to countless dangers, how their only beauty is in their feathers, their nimble flight and their warblings. But is their flight, so effortless to the watching eye, a gruesome toil? And are their warblings cries of pain, harsh ejaculations born of greed and fear and hatred? Bah! I know that man flies safer and with greater ease, and that he makes finer feathers for his smooth skin, and that his mind can fashion songs, to which the dull chatter of birds is as the croaking of a frog to a tune by Beethoven, or a sonnet by Shakespeare.

In search of truth, I went forth on the rocks by the seashore of a wild island, with the mind of a primitive savage, because I had slept well and looked on life with the unreasoning acceptance of a man, dancing in the morning, before the sun on a Pacific island shore. To feed on fruits and fish, to dance and sing and fornicate, get children and then die. No truth, to us, who have tasted the delicious wines of philosophy and science and the arts. We have climbed too many mountains to take delight by the marsh, even though it be Samoan, or off the Breton coast in summer. And yet, sufficient for truth is the reality thereof.

In any case, what means we? Why not I? What pleasure is it to me to be told by a sociologist that man is a social animal? That as an animal he must eat, drink and be protected against the elements and lust for union with his opposite in sex? And that because he is social he must build cities and struggle towards godliness by enlarging the scope of his intellect? But there it is. Damn their eyes! They have me by the throat.

What did I do? I slipped off my shoes and stood in a shallow pool, the bottom of which was covered with yellow moss. As my feet pressed on the moss, the water oozed from it and swirled from beneath my feet in foam. My legs trembled by contact with the cold brine. The cold became intense, until I could endure it no longer. I had to leap from the pool on to the dry rock, on which I stamped vigorously, in order to heat my chilled legs. I laughed as I stamped and recalled how I once stood under an ice-cold fountain in the Wicklow mountains. The fountain leaped from a rocky gorge between two trees whose branches intertwined and dropped the long tails of the plants that fed on them into the white arc of the fountain. The strands of parasite plants floated there like fishing lines and I stood in the dark pool below, now and again thrusting my head forward into the fountain. At each thrust I shouted, stung by the cold of the water, and then I leaped to a rock on which the sun was shining and I came near to fainting with joy. Pride of life! "Why evolve, then, from anything to anything? Truth, you slippery whore, your face changes at every second when I try to read it with my mind. I can only see one face and you have a myriad of them. Then, lay off, mind and eat your porridge in a corner, you boor. You are not fit to sit on this whore's couch. Her thighs'll have none of your black-fingered groping. Ho! She's only heated by the lance of beauty, straight from the loins of life. I take what I can get and never ask who pricked the bubble of her virtue."

And there I saw upon the low-tide shore, where the sea-bed was a yellow swamp of languid weeds, the hordes of Ghenghiz Khan, laying waste cities, because that lord preferred smooth pastures to a pile of bricks. I saw the shuffle of his skulking camels over the plain and the mad gallop of his shouting horsemen, putting to the sword philosophers. I saw this because I had slept well and the sun shone upon the sea and the fermented air of the morning was flowing to my lungs. Had I arisen with a bile, to look upon a cloudy sky and misty earth, I might have seen Pythagoras sitting among the yellow weeds, preaching brotherly love.

At first glance it is a torture to admit that for me there is no difference in worth between Ghenghiz and Pythagoras, although the one ravaged civilization with fire and sword, while the other strove to make men live in gentle peace with one another, raising the temple of divinity. In spite of that, I shout that I am no philosopher, but a vessel into which life pours sweet wine or vinegar, from a hand that is indifferently careless. Wine or vinegar, I must accept and drink it to the dregs.

Very often, what one thinks is vinegar, proves to be the best wine. When I arrived at Caterham barracks as a recruit, it seemed to me that, of my own volition, I had been condemned to hell. At the barrack gates I heard the sergeant of the guard yell at a sentry who was remiss in saluting an officer. And then I was led across the square to the room reserved for recruits newly arrived. All the way I heard fierce shouting, and the men who passed moved like automata, rigid, with inhuman expressions, carrying weapons like brigands. I passed that night numb with horror of the future; horrified by the coarse beings who had joined the same day as myself as much as by the inhuman rigidity and ferocious language of those already trained as soldiers. The war I was going to wage against a powerful enemy was remote and unreal. Its dangers were devoured by the horrors of this school in which I was to be trained in the art of killing.

After a frightful night, I paraded next morning to get my kit. The rough uniform was handed out to me by a cynical fellow who winked at me and said: "Well, matey, how d'ye like yer Flanders burial shroud?" I was stripped of every garment of my civilian state. My head was shorn. My feet were put in heavy boots in which I could scarcely walk. Carrying my bag of kit I was led away, a crude yokel, to the hut where I was to live while being trained. And lo! once I was dressed as a soldier, I lost my individuality and became like the other recruits, whose foul curses and stinking bodies had horrified me on the previous night. Now it made no difference whether they had worked under the earth as miners, or as navvies in sewers, and that I could write Greek verse. We were all timid human beings, looking alike because we were dressed alike, and crude yokels because we were untrained in the art of soldiering. "Throw down your kit here, rookey. That's your bed." At night a drunken recruit, cocky because he was in his seventh week, said the bed was his and that I would have to find another one. He had just come out of clink. I took my bag and sat near the stove. I was too timid to complain. A soldier who sat there, smoking a last cigarette before turning into his bed, looked at me and said: "Hey, mate, ye're here to learn how to fight, so ye might as well begin. Slosh that Dago in the kisser. Get after him, son. Let's see have ye got any Irish guts." The man smiled, and I liked his two fine rows of white teeth and the way his cropped hair lay in a straight row on his forehead like a ram. I jumped up, went over to the man who lay on my bed and told him to get off it. He was a big man with black moustaches and a bronzed face, because he had lived many years in the Argentine as a cowboy. Cursing in Spanish, he got to his feet. I shot out my left hand and caught him on the point of the jaw and he went down like a log. He got up again, squared himself groggily, and I sent him down once more, with a blow on the same spot. He was knocked out and lay on the floor groaning. The men in the hut began to shout: "Well done, rookey." But the trained soldier in charge of us called from his bed in the far corner: "Hey there, you crummy lot o' bastards, what's all this row about? Come here, potboy, or whatever you were before you went to live in Wormwood Scrubbs. What d'ye mean by fighting in the barrack room? You're for small reports in the morning."

I got two pack drills for the offence and I had to fight the Dago with gloves in the gymnasium ring the following evening and was knocked out by him in the first round. Yet the episode did me a great deal of good, together with winning me the friendship of the Dago, who tried unsuccessfully to teach me how to make use of the punch I carried in my left hand.

Slowly and painfully I suffered the process of being changed from a civilian to a soldier, particularly to a guardsman; for even in wartime the brigade did not relax its iron discipline of training, or its meticulousness in the choice of its human material. I learned in my humble way *les grandeurs et misères de la vie militaire*. Little by little the vinegar turned into wine. The foulmouthedness of the corporal who trained my squad lost its horror and I saw his fine humanity beneath his rough and brutal exterior. I who had until then worshipped the mind to the extent of neglecting the body, now worshipped the body to the neglect of the mind. I who had lived alone, brooding on ideas and suspicious of association with other youths unless they had the same interest in ideas as myself, was now forced to become the mate and equal of all and sundry. A rebel from my childhood, I was forced to accept authority, and soon I found that it was a relief and an ennoblement to click my heels and salute instead of being a debasement and an insult to my pride. I learned to despise civilians because they did not carry their bodies or discipline their lives with the same nobility as soldiers. I despised them especially by comparison with soldiers who were sworn by an oath of honour to give up their lives, if the necessity arose to do so, in defence of an ideal.

You sneer, you damned pacifists and hunchbacked, snarling curs, at this expression of love for the profession that so far has been considered the most noble, because it brought out in the highest degree the two virtues of valour and discipline. What is your argument? Drivel about cannon fodder and hired murderers to defend the loot of financiers. The horse cannot choose his rider. His noble back bears the miscreant as well as the virtuous. "Sergeant! Put them in the cells and flog them and let's get on with our story."

It's not a soldier's business whether he is sworn to defend a king, or a republican president, or the executive committee of a communist party, or the mangy cattle of an African tribe against a prowling lion. For us it was first and foremost the honour of the regiment and of the brigade that we felt sworn to defend.

They used to say in Caterham: "You'll go out this gate a corpse or a guardsman." And to my mind it would be a good thing in life that all individuals who could not be trained into guardsmen should become corpses. If society is sick and if mankind is in danger of being forced to retire from its attack on that wall it has set out to scale, it is largely because those who are too cowardly or too degenerate to bear arms and suffer the discipline of a soldier's life are allowed to take part in government. Indeed, I can think of no fitter punishment for many men in public life to-day than to place them with their toes to a concrete wall and force them to do rifle drill until they could slope arms without tearing the skin off their knuckles.

And to what purpose was that training? In this book I set out to shame the devil, first with my sins and secondly with the declaration of one virtue, that I do love humanity. And I claim that it is to my training as a soldier I owe the flowering of that love. Without it and without having taken part in the great holocaust of the war, I might have grown into a barren scholar, or a warped æsthete, a pretty pedlar of emasculated thought, like those who failed to hear the bugle sound "stand to your arms." When? At any time. Socrates got the prize for valour at Potidæa. Sophocles served as a hoplite. Tolstoy was at the siege of Sebastopol. Those who shine out most brightly as apostles of peace and human brotherhood in their writings are those who kept their rendezvous with death and were respited. Cervantes also fought and lived to sing of laughter.

We have had our grouch. Now let us boast of war. Now I look upon my training as a soldier as a preparation for taking part in the great drama of a new god being born. My journey from Caterham depot to the trenches was the first act in this drama and my journey from London to this island on the Breton coast was the last act, explaining the meaning of the piece. Salvation!

I landed at Le Havre at dawn in winter and marched through the town in bitter cold, which numbed the lobes of my ears and the fingers that clutched my slung weapon. Up to Harfleur we went and camped there; a spot of which Shakespeare sang. We crowded into little tents and then waited, restlessly, like actors in the wings waiting their cues. At last it came, the order for the front. We were placed on a train and carried towards the line. The train moved very slowly, as in a slow march, a ceremonial march for those who were doomed to die, to be offered up on the altar of the new god. At last we came within earshot of the guns. Their mournful booming was like a signal for our silence now that we approached the sacred precincts of the place of sacrifice. And silence fell on us, and in our eyes there was a startled look, the look of bulls who rush from their black pens into the lurid sunshine of the arena, the look of gladiators crying: " Ave, Cæsar! Morituri te salutant."

Through the heavy mud, we marched from the railhead to a camp and were detailed to our platoons. I entered my appointed hut and sat down and looked with awe at the men who were sitting there on their madedown beds, picking vermin from their clothes. Their heads were shorn bare. Their faces were wan and their eyes had the strained look of bulls, behind whose shoulders the lance of the picador has made its gash. A doomed look. I felt the foulness of death creeping towards my body, and my clean flesh recoiled from the foulness, but in vain.

Now I marched once more, but this time I marched in a dead man's place. A hole had been made in the ranks by death and I filled the hole. Beside me were men who had been in action when the hole was made. I was a new patch on an old garment. What awful silence beneath the booming of the guns! What darkness in spite of the wild light of the demon stars that sprang from the shattered earth as shells exploded. And then there was no road, but a long, thin line of boards, stretched on the smelly mud. All round this narrow line, the pock-faced land, bereft of life, was walking, as they say in doss-houses, with vermin of all breeds, and like a deserted market, it was littered with the weapons and the stores and the clothes and the equipment of the dead, who were also there, rotting in the naked night, without the decency of fire or burial. We burrow in the earth, and stumble through a long tunnel until we reach the line. Now we are face to face with the enemy. He also has come up, after having stood with his toes against a concrete wall, doing rifle drill until he could slope arms without knocking the skin off his knuckles. He is standing there in some dead man's place, doomed for the sacrifice. Beyond our wire and his, he is crouching in his trench, listening, his shorn head, like mine, encasing a tortured, ignorant mind; and yet a noble man, because he has taken the oath of valour and of discipline.

And there we stayed, fighting one another from either side the walls of barbed wire, fighting on the ground and under the ground and in the air, hurling steel and flame and gas at one another, until one day I saw a banner hoisted over the trench of the enemy and on the banner was written: "Workers of the world unite." The new god had been born. That was the end of the first act, the rising in the east of the star of revolution. The vinegar of death was changed into the wine of life.

The second act was our revolt and the defeat of our revolt; not only the defeat of my revolt, but of the revolt of all men in western Europe who had seen the light and failed to reach it because of their weariness and the strength of the chains that bound them. But what does it matter now that I have turned aside, to become a cynic, a fornicator and a tavern set. The fire was damped but it still burned under its covering of wet slack. On the rake, my boys. Then coal the bars and get up steam. We put to sea again.

## XV

A POET must understand the truth before he can create poetry, but he must forget it before he can release the energy necessary to sing his song. In other words, he must love what he is going to write, and yet the love must be so intense and so full of fire that it lacks all sense, both of possession and of responsibility. It is a lust rather than that spiritual love of which the priests and nuns, of Christianity and of emasculated literature, preach to us about. At least, it was as a lust that the creative impulse returned to me that morning on the island, while I floundered about among the yellow weeds, on which I had a few minutes before seen the hordes of Ghenghiz Khan.

It was the story I had tried to write in Concarneau that came to my hand. Now it was no effort to write it. It rushed out of its own accord. The words danced to my piping. The rhythm flowed without interruption, finding its own balance without needing my direction. And as soon as I began to write it, my youth returned. I felt young and potent like a young colt in full gallop over a sunny field in early morning. But it had nothing to do with truth, if truth lies hidden in the social shibboleths about which I had been raving. Now they were nothing more than the cries of pain of a pregnant woman, " sound and fury, signifying nothing." I lost all sense of time and place, all feeling that there was an objective to be striven for in life, that I was at times a drunkard and a lecher, that I had lost my typewriter in Paris and had failed to win a lot of money at the races, that I was in debt and that the mouth of a child was dependant on my labour for food.

By the functioning of this triumphant lust, I became detached from the material world, except for the pencil and the paper I used. I sat on a rock by the shore and wrote until I had covered all the paper in my notebook with words. The sun rose in the heavens without my heeding it. My stomach cried for food without my heeding it. My bare feet, crusted with brine water, got scorched by the sun and smarted, but I felt no pain. When at last I had no more paper on which to write, I stared at the ground, smiling foolishly and feeling exhausted like a man who had run for miles. And then, I suddenly remembered everything and burst into tears.

It was the first time I had wept for many years out of gentleness, and they were tears of joy, for I felt completely humiliated. It was made manifest to me that what was evil in my nature came from my shame of being humble and innocent; that this shame of humility and innocence from time to time had turned the wine of my imagination into vinegar, so that I spat like a horrid cat and snarled instead of singing gently like a lark, which asks no reward for his song from those who hear it. Even my confessions were hypocrisy, for they were made in arrogance, as by one who wishes to make plain to all men that he can go naked without fear of mankind's mud staining his nakedness.

To make my humiliation complete, I tore what I had written into shreds and dropped the morsels into the tide that was flowing back and forth, hoisting up the yellow weeds and then dropping them insolently, like the crowns of mighty kings deposed by death among devouring worms. And when I had done so, my tears became bitter, and almost at once they dried, and I saw that even the joy of humiliation was denied to me. I realized that I would have to go on selling my soul for bread.

"Pick up those scraps of paper. See that little scrap there that has drifted high and dry on the edge of a rock, the pencilled words almost obliterated by the tide. One word is still legible. It is the word malodorous. Yah! It is the label of your past and the forecast of your future. Ill-born dog, whether you whine, or howl, or bark with loving joy, you are still a dog to be kicked. Gap-toothed clown, go down on your belly and crawl before the throne of mammon. Otherwise you'll get no bread. Call yourself lucky for having the ear of his doorkeeper and being allowed to hang about his court. There are far better men starving beyond the walls."

I hurried back to the house. It was almost noon, as I had been writing for many hours, just to produce that one word malodorous, which stank in my mind, even though it was already washed off the paper by the tide. Nothing was left of my thoughtless joy, or of my ecstasy of creation except that loathsome word, and I felt so despondent that I had not even courage to enter the house and ask for food. I leaned against the wall of the *vivier*, stared at the ground and again thought of suicide, but I shuddered and dismissed the thought at once. Not death but love was what I now wanted. A shoulder to weep upon. Yes, to weep without shame and without tears, to weep into the well of my soul and heal its wounds with their salt. Then I roused myself with an effort and thought how artificial and cowardly my sorrow was, considering that I had money still in my pocket, that I could purchase food and a bed and get back to London, where I could find work, selling my writings.

In order to give force to this argument, I recalled how I had twelve years ago walked up and down outside a bakeshop in the East India Dock road, ravenously hungry, staring greedily at the cakes in the window each time I passed and yet too intimidated by hunger to go in and ask for a cake, or break a pane of glass, grab a handful and run away. What if I were caught and put in prison for housebreaking and theft? I would be fed and housed in prison. It was not fear of prison and the duress of its life that held me back, but some weight of shame that lay too heavily on my will. I walked away, getting more and more hungry, until I found some institution which I entered and tried to ask the clergyman in charge for a shilling in order to wire to my sister for money. I waited in the place for an hour, but could not find in myself enough courage to ask the clergyman. He shuffled about the room, being professionally gay and chatting with the poor wretches, who fawned on him with the horrible and degrading fawning of the destitute. When he approached me and put me a few questions about my position, I replied arrogantly and bridled up at the insolence of his manner. My hunger ceased to sting. But when he took his hat and left the building, I was on the verge of hysterics. I went out and wandered about the streets until nightfall, when I found myself in Greenwich. Not having slept at all during the previous night and having fasted for twenty-four hours or more, I was utterly exhausted and I lay down in the shelter of a blank wall in a laneway.

It began to rain and I was soon drenched to the skin. I got up and staggered away from my shelter, which was indeed no shelter but a place to lie in peace. It was a winter's night and bitterly cold. I began to shiver, and at the same time it seemed that my body was on fire. I was in a fever. I came across a watchman who was guarding a bit of road that was being mended. He was sitting in his little box and there was a glowing brazier in front of him. He was eating bread and cheese and drinking tea from a quart can, from which he pulled back the lid with his thumb every time he took a sip. I watched him, standing a little distance away, in the doorway of a shop. He finished his bread and cheese, rolled up the paper on which they had lain, wiped his knife on the leg of his trousers, closed it and put it in his pocket. Then he drained the last of the tea, shook the can and threw the used leaves into the brazier. The fire smoked a little and the flames ran sideways for a moment. Then the man took his pipe, pressed down the tobacco in the bowl, made a spill with the paper he had rolled and lit it at the brazier.

I watched every movement the man made with a fierce intensity, as if I wished to lose myself in him. Even the desire to ask him for food or permission to share with him the heat of his brazier had left me. I am certain that if he had offered to share his food and his heat with me, I would have felt offended and have walked away arrogantly, using the last remnant of my strength to maintain the shadow of my pride. My pride or my loneliness?

The man got out of his hut and looked about him. He raised the edge of a tarpaulin that covered some heap of things beside the hut. I was afraid he might see me standing in the doorway and talk to me, so I wandered along the street, in the opposite direction from his hut. I sheltered in another doorway. I could no longer stand, so I lay down and closed my eyes. I could make no further effort. Then I felt at peace and ceased to suffer, either from hunger, or want of sleep, or fever. I dare say that if I had not been interfered with I would have died happily in the doorway, for during the time I lay there I had wonderful dreams of my childhood. Nor did I fear death, for nothing held me to life.

However, a policeman came along just about dawn and roused me.

"Who are you? What are you doing here?" he cried, flashing his torch in my face.

When I could speak I told him that I had paid off a ship in Cardiff and that I had gone to Southampton looking for a ship to New York, but had been unable to find one before my money was spent. Then I came back to London.

"Well! You can't stay there," he said kindly. "Get up an' we'll see what's to be done."

I tried to get to my feet, but fell prone on the pavement and became unconscious. I woke up in the workhouse infirmary to which they had brought me. In a week I had recovered and a lady visitor gave me a shilling to telegraph for money. I left the infirmary and went to Jack's Palace to look for an Australian who was down and out. He had shared with me the last meal I had eaten before going into the infirmary. I found him and collected about twenty other men who were destitute and took them all into an eating-house, where we ate bacon and eggs until we could eat no more. And then I went home to Ireland.

However! It was no use recalling that incident, as I leaned against the wall of the *vivier*, for at that moment I could not decide whether it was better to lie in the doorway with a fever, dreaming about my childhood and resigned to death, than to eat with destitute men and feel the joy of giving. Was my relationship with the night watchman better or worse than my relationship with the men I had fed? Was it better to drift through the streets of London, homeless and penniless, avoiding human contact, in complete loneliness, until death should come from exhaustion, than to strive for success, to do one's duty, whatever that is, and to be hearty?

"Good Lord!" I thought. "I have made no progress whatsoever in the last ten years, since I began to write.

I still have a grievance, whereas I should be free from all malice. It was not pride that made me recoil from asking the clergyman for a shilling, or the night watchman for the heat of his fire, or the woman of this house for food. It was and is really malice, to make them responsible for some imaginary wrong that has been inflicted on me by society. Imaginary, I say imaginary and stress the word, because wrong cannot be inflicted on one as an artist, there being no universal criterion of good and evil by which the artist can separate those experiences that are positive from those that are negative. Ha! I get closer to it. Am I acting a part? Was I acting a part that night, when I stood in the doorway with a fever, looking at the man eating bread and cheese? Playing the outcast? Am I now acting the same part, even though I have no fever and I have money? Whose money? Why have I made this journey? Is it really a simple expedition to recoup my health? That is what a normal person would call it, but I insist on giving it a very complex and extraordinary significance, in order to get a complex and extraordinary value from it. I make a mountain out of a mole-hill deliberately. Come. Silence and act another part, or else . . . what happens?"

I saw a malign eye looking at me from a distance. It was the eye of a snake I had seen on a rock by the bank of a little river south of Rio de Janeiro. He was coiled on the rock and he mesmerized me, but I sat quite still when he raised his head. What pride and glorious arrogance there was in the pose of his upraised neck! A malign eye, but no more malign than mine which looked into his, with the same pride and arrogance. For a few moments he stared and then slid away into the grass, and I felt terribly afraid. I was not afraid of him, but of my own eye, which I had not known until then to be the eye of a snake. With my eye I had made him slide into the grass, and with the same eye, even in the most exalted moments of the last ten years, I have looked on life and sought for beauty in the taking of it. Ask a shuffling, babbling, hypocritical parson for a shilling, or a brute night watchman for his brazier's heat? Bah! Destroy them with a glance, or crawl into the grass, to die of my dismemberment, by the sword of my passions.

I saw that eye from afar and I knew it was no good my trying to fly from it. Even on a desert island it would be there, now distant, now by my side, having sport with me. Such being the case, I must face it boldly and try to put it in harness. The wild horse of the pampas can be tamed and put to a gentle use, once it has been made to answer the curb and accept the authority of its rider's knees against its sides.

I looked up and saw Pol and Antoine approaching the jetty in their row boats. They had been out all morning with their nets. I went down to meet them. We took the nets out of the boat. They were very pleased, because they had taken several mullet. I bought two of the fish from them and then we went to the bar to drink. Pierre and his brother Jean with us. They also had had a good morning's fishing and we all talked in loud voices, with the gaiety of simple folk, who are in direct dependance on the bounty of nature; gay when the earth and sea give plentifully, sad and silent when their yield is poor.

And I thought:

"This is the end of my journey. I have been to hell and now I may rise again. This little Pol, the fisherman, has put me to shame. He mourns the loss of his wife, but he still goes on fishing, and he is pleased when he finds some gleaming mullet in his net. He did not cut them into shreds and cast them back into the sea once more. He smiles and drinks in thanksgiving. How true it is what Dostoieffsky said, that the more a man concerns himself with generalizations about love for all humanity and setting aright whatever he finds wrong in the construction of human society, the less love he has to waste on his friends and dependants and those with whom he comes directly in contact during his daily life. Like the Christian missionaries who go to far China with their gospel and are blind to the cries for help of those poor wretches that are living in slums near their own doors, like Rousseau who deserted his children in order to write a book about their proper upbringing, I have gone mooching in search of truth, while shutting my eyes to it wherever I met it. To work, laggard. Whether it's fishing for mullet, or writing the Iliad, work is the only thing that can really satisfy."

So I drank and ate my mullet and potatoes and went out on the beach, where I stripped off my clothes and slept. Then I swam along the shore and ran upon the sand and sang a song. When the sun began to sink in the west, I took another notebook and began my story once more. The word malodorous no longer stank in my mind. Here is what I wrote.

## XVI

### "THE CARESS"

WITH a sudden movement of his arm, Delaney raised his pint and drank, until the stout had sunk into the mass of froth that lay at the bottom of the glass. Then he shuddered and let his arms hang loose, forward from his stooping shoulders, in the attitude of a man beginning to get drunk. The glass canted forward. The froth poured forth on to the earthen floor, where it made a brownish pool, decked with golden bubbles that swelled and burst. He raised his head. His eyes had grown dim and bloodshot.

"I want to marry a young girl," he cried in a harsh tone. "I'll have Mary Madigan or nobody at all."

Pat McDonagh, a tall, handsome man with curly golden hair, sitting opposite Delaney on a low stool, laughed and said:

"Well, that settles it. There's no more to be said."

"Sure," said Delaney. "I'm fifty years of age, but I'm able to make children yet. I want children. If I marry Kate Cody, she's forty if she's a year, where would I get children? She's dry like an old shoe. I want a young girl like Mary Madigan. Come with me, neighbours, in God's name, and ask her for me."

He began to perspire. Ordinarily a silent and modest

fellow, drink had made him garrulous and somewhat repulsive. His cap was at the back of his head, the peak upright from his forehead and to one side. His hair was almost white, yet his face had the innocence and freshness of youth, a sort of virginal expression that looked incongruous for a man of his age. His cheeks were as rosy as those of a young girl. His mouth and nose were well shaped. He had fine eyes. Yet he was dry and withered "like an old shoe," as he said himself. He was not dry and withered because of his age, but because he had never known the joy and exuberance of passion granted its fulfilment in action. His whole lank body, all hunched and twisted by hard work in the fields, told the same tale of frustration as his face; lean and hungry and unkempt, like a tree whose growth had been arrested by a sudden drought of the earth about its roots. The joints of his big toes bulged out like great thorns through his rawhide shoes.

"Go your own road," said Dan O'Brien, a squat, powerful man with a bald forehead, who sat beside Delaney on the form, "though you'd be a wiser man to take my advice and marry Kate Cody. She's yours for the asking. How do you know she can't have children? Nobody has tried her nest for eggs. They may be there in plenty, and chickens too, if she had a good cock on her roost. How do you know you'd have children by Mary Madigan? Look at Pat McDonagh there. He's a fine man and his wife is a neat schooner of a woman, fore an' aft, without a tear in her full rig, but he has no children."

O'Brien laughed, fondling his pint between his thighs. McDonagh leaned forward and struck him a heavy blow on the chest. The blow resounded, hollow as on a drum.

"Curse you," said McDonagh, "you think because you have six sons that you are a better man than me. Change wives and I'll show you. No matter how good the bait may be, the fisherman comes home empty if there are no fish."

O'Brien laughed and pulled McDonagh towards him by the shoulders. They kissed one another drunkenly on the cheeks.

"I want to marry a young girl," cried Delaney once more. "Are ye coming with me, neighbours?"

"Yes," they answered, "we'll come with you, Bartly."

"Give me three bottles of whisky," Delaney said to the tavern-keeper.

"Three bottles, you devil," said O'Brien. "Is it for the wedding an' all?"

"Three bottles," said Delaney. "It would be only one if I went after Kate Cody, but Mary Madigan is another story entirely. I'll show her there's money in my purse."

"More power to you," said McDonagh, nudging O'Brien.

The two of them winked at one another and giggled behind their hands while Delaney counted out the money from his purse. Then each put a bottle under his jersey and they left the tavern. They turned west along the road to Portoona. They were all fairly drunk. It was a summer's evening and there was a fresh breeze blowing from the sea. The freshness of the air made them dizzy.

They staggered slightly. Delaney began to sing in a harsh, cracked voice.

"Keep quiet," said McDonagh, " or you'll get no wife to-night, for you'll lie beaten in the barracks."

"I want to marry a young girl," Delaney cried.

Then he walked on in silence. He looked ridiculous in his incipient drunkenness, uttering such a cry. When he walked, drunk in that way, his premature old age was more apparent. He was like one of those returned emigrants one often sees, fellows who worked ten years or more in American factories that sucked their blood.

Opposite the post-office a young man, who sat on a wall, saluted McDonagh and said:

"Going home, Pat?"

"Come west with us a bit," McDonagh said.

"I'm satisfied," the young man said.

He jumped lightly from the wall and fell into step beside McDonagh. His name was Martin Derrane. For three years he had been serving as a soldier and he was now returned to our village, where he lived with his aunt. Although it was nine months since his return and he had long since spent all his money, he showed no inclination to look for work, but talked vaguely of going to America. He was extremely handsome, very slim and dark, with splendid white teeth and eyes of a peculiar intensity.

They were a fine sight, those three young men, all in their prime and fashioned with an elegance which is, alas, much too rare in nature. McDonagh towered above the other two, his golden curls drooping over his forehead. Their arms and legs swung in rhythm and their hips moved from side to side in unison. Their shoulders, held level and rigid, jerked with each step. Women turned in the road to look after them as they marched west, with the red glow of the setting sun upon their bronzed faces.

Delaney, plunging along behind, looked like their servant; and yet, poor man, his thoughts were full of conceit. He felt certain that the beautiful Mary Madigan would be his betrothed before morning.

"Huh!" he muttered to himself. "They wanted to bring me to Kate Cody's house. She's a good worker, is she? What's that to me? I can do all the work that's needed. I want a young girl between sheets. I want children. I've been long enough a lonely slave of the land."

They did not speak until they were some distance west of the village. Then they turned into a narrow lane and sat under a fence. Delaney took the bottle from his jersey and drew the cork. They each drank two rounds. The bottle was empty.

"My soul from the devil!" Delaney cried. "There's one of them gone. Two bottles are not enough for that house."

"Devil roast you," McDonagh said. "Can't you get potheen at the sheebeen?"

"All the same," said O'Brien, "it's a shame to have a man spend all his money and he maybe not going to get the girl after all."

"What house are ye heading for?" young Derrane said.

"Madigan's house, you devil," McDonagh said. "You should know it well, you young dog, for you're often nosing on that scent."

Delaney looked suspiciously at young Derrane. Derrane frowned at McDonagh and said in a surly tone:

"Which daughter are ye after? The eldest one, Julia?"

"Julia!" shouted Delaney. "I'd rather lie with a corpse. No, son. It's Mary I'll bring to the altar. I have thirty acres of land and plenty of stock and money in the bank. So I'll get her. Come, neighbours. Strike the road, in God's name. The night is falling."

He went in front with O'Brien. Derrane walked in the rear with McDonagh.

"Look here, Pat," he whispered angrily. "I'll not go with ye."

"Why so?" said McDonagh.

"Devil roast his bones!" said Derrane viciously. "Hasn't he the impudence to cast eyes on the most beautiful girl in the parish?"

"What do we care?" said McDonagh. "We'll get a good night out of him."

"Well, I care a lot," said Derrane. "I love her. That's why."

"Then why don't you ask her yourself?"

"How could I? I haven't a penny."

"What does that matter?" said McDonagh. "She ought to have money. She was six years in America, earning good wages, and she's a steady girl. Make up to her and take her with you to America. She'll pay your passage if she cares for you. Come on with us, man. To-night is your chance to have a word with her. You can slip out with her into the yard when everybody is drunk and careless. Have sense, man. Sure, I'd rather you'd have her than an old devil like Delaney. Aren't you my second cousin, eh?"

"Thanks, Pat," said Derrane, gripping McDonagh's hand.

They hurried and joined the others. Delaney had now become very garrulous.

"When my mother died last year," he said, "I had two hundred pounds in the bank. Now there's only eighty pounds left, but that should last me out until my marriage. When a man is raking round after a wife, he's every scoundrel's pet. Dry mouths and empty pockets gather round him like flies."

McDonagh nudged Derrane and winked. Derrane scowled.

"Seventy pounds all told it cost me to chase after that young girl from Inishtual," said Delaney.

"You'd be better off to leave the young girls alone and look for a serious person of your age," said O'Brien.

"Seventy pounds!" said McDonagh, in a tone of pretended horror. "It's a fortune for a poor land slave to spend."

"Seventy pounds in all it cost me," shouted Delaney, "and for that much I didn't even squeeze her in my arms. It was robbery."

"How was it robbery?" said O'Brien. "You fool, you deserved all you got."

"All the same," said Delaney, "it wasn't fair. I caught sight of her on the steamer going into the town last November and she looked fine; red and juicy like an orange. God! She brought water to my mouth. Her brother and her uncle were with her, so I made up to them, and when we landed, we drank together. John Hernon from my place was there, so I gave him the word while we were at the back of the house and he drew down the talk of marriage. He put it fair and square, how I didn't care for a portion. Thirty acres of land and money saved. What did I want with a girl's portion? Only her flesh and blood and the harvest of her womb. Cripes! The brother and the uncle said they were well satisfied. They said this and that, we drank for days and the money flew. Back I came home from the mainland. I got a boat and a crew and I went to Inishtual with a keg of whisky. We spent a week on that island and we drank nearly all that was on it, but all the while I never got any nearer to the girl than a goat to Heaven on the Day of Judgment. I came home empty and the tally was seventy pounds."

"Ah! God help you, poor man," said McDonagh in mock sorrow. "Let's sit under this wall and have another drink to drown the memory of what you spent."

"Let's go on," said O'Brien. "We're drunk enough as it is. We can't go footless into Madigan's house."

Now it was night, but the full moon was up and it was almost as bright as day. They sang an odd stave as they walked, clasping hands and stumbling, one against the other. As they were passing a field close by Portoona strand, a young mare put her head over the fence and whinnied.

"That's my little mare," McDonagh said. "She's faster on the road than a diving gannet. Let's take her on the strand for a bit. We'd be too early yet at Madigan's house."

He knocked a gap in the fence and took the mare's halter from beneath a stone. He put it on her head and led her on to the road.

"God! She's lovely!" said O'Brien.

He caressed her haunches. The young mare shivered as his hand passed gently down her glistening, black hide. Her wide, silken nostrils twitched and she pawed the road with her fore hooves, one after the other. Her long tail lashed her sides. Her head, curved inwards to her neck by the drawn halter, edged from side to side, struggling to break loose. Her great eyes looked frightened. She was afraid of these drunken men who crowded round her, talking in loud tones and staggering. She sniffed at the strange odour of alcohol from their breath and felt afraid.

"Get up on her, Pat," said Derrane. "We'll see who can turn her shortest at full gallop on the sand."

"I'm satisfied," McDonagh said. "Hold her head. She's nervous in the night."

They held her head and whispered to her. She tried to rear as McDonagh leaped on her back.

"We have no time to race her on the strand,' grumbled Delaney. "They'll be snug in bed before we reach the house unless we hurry."

"Have you no shame in you?" said Derrane. "Can't you be quiet?"

"You son of a loose mother," shouted Delaney, "you want her yourself."

He rushed at Derrane with clenched fists. O'Brien came between them.

"Keep quiet," he said, " or I'll beat the two of you."

They jostled about, the three of them, shouting. The mare took fright and reared. McDonagh loosed the halter, touched her on the side of the neck with his palm and leaned forward over her ears. Then he yelled.

The mare gasped and shot forward like a stone from a catapult. Her four steel-shod hooves swept from the hard road with a scraping sound and then you could only see her tail, spread like a black fan behind her, in the cloud of sandy dust she raised as she ran west. The men on the road ceased jostling. They answered McDonagh's yell, excited by the mare's glorious running in the moonlight. Then they followed her down to the strand.

"Let's not delay here," said Delaney, when they reached the sand. "It's time we were at Madigan's house."

"God's curse on your hurry," said O'Brien. "Let's ride this lovely mare first on the sand. Christ in Paradise! No swallow ever drank the wind as fast as she."

Swinging the long halter about his curly head, McDonagh turned the mare at the far end of the strand and then rode back along the sea's edge where the low tide was frothing gently among the moonlit pebbles. Down there the hooves hardly made a sound and you could hear the mare's breath in the distance, coming in sudden gusts, like the sound a thumping dashboard makes in a full, closed churn. Then she halted, panting, and McDonagh dismounted. The other two gathered round her. Delaney went up near the road and sat on a rock. He felt angry.

"They don't care whether I get her or not," he said

to himself. "They only want to spend my money and get a good night's drinking out of me."

As he looked at the three beautiful young men down there on the sand about the dancing mare, all tense with youth's wild energy, carousing in the moonlight by the murmuring sea, he felt enraged at his own impotence. He saw his youth misspent and barren of pleasure, a callow lout who feared to look a woman in the eyes, his widowed mother's pet, looking askance, with brutish disapproval, on all amusement, as temptations of the devil and shameless extravagance. Then his mother died. He was alone. A wife became necessary.

Then for six months he had scoured the island for a bride, unseemly like a rampant goat, which at the fall of autumn goes abroad upon the crags, malodorous, to leap on all and sundry with a wailing cry, in which there is a forecast of bleak death.

"Blood in ounce," he muttered. "It took me twenty years to gather that two hundred pounds and I've spent nearly all of it in six months, making a fool of myself with lads that are only laughing at me."

He jumped to his feet, suddenly determined to go home and leave them. But immediately he thought of Mary Madigan.

"I'll stay," he said fiercely. "When I'm married to her the whole island will see that I am a man as good as ever was bred here. I'll be nobody's fool to be laughed at."

This thought gave him a wild courage.

"Come on," he shouted, "or I'll get better men than ye to come along."

At that moment young Derrane, mounted on the mare, dashed west along the sand, by the sea's edge, where red weeds were glistening in the moonlight on the white shore. He yelled and swung the halter about his head. Delaney picked up a pebble and threw it savagely after the mare. It fell with a dull thud into the sea.

"Hey!" cried McDonagh. "What are you throwing stones at?"

"Come on, I say," shouted Delaney. "If ye don't want to come, I'll get other men. I have the money. I'm not depending on ye."

"Devil take your money," said O'Brien. "Come down and ride this mare."

"I don't want your mare," said Delaney. "I have a mare of my own. I'll fight the three of you. I'm a man as good as ever was bred on this island. Come on. You're trying to make a fool of me. I'll show you what I am."

He began to strip off his clothes.

"We had better humour the poor devil," said O'Brien. "He's so hot on the scent that he's out of his mind."

"Devil take him," said McDonagh. "We have the two bottles. Let him go if he wants to go."

"All the same," said O'Brien, "let's humour him. We'll have fun at Madigan's and we might get a gallon of potheen out of him as well."

"It's more likely we'll get hot water thrown on us, coming with an old ram like that," said McDonagh.

They tittered and stumbled against one another. They went over to Delaney and took hold of him and flattered him. He struggled in their powerful arms, but he soon grew calm and forgot his anger. Each of them took him by an arm and they marched west with him.

They saw the mare trotting towards them, riderless, with her halter trailing on the sand.

"Blood in ounce!" said McDonagh. "Martin Derrane is thrown."

"So he is," said O'Brien. "Look at him stretched unconscious over there."

"Ho! The devil mend him!" said Delaney. "I'd rather that than two fat bullocks."

O'Brien began to run towards Derrane. McDonagh caught the mare and pulled her after him.

"I hope he broke his blasted neck," said Delaney, as he floundered after them through the sand.

They found Derrane stretched limp, face downwards. They raised him and poured some whisky down his throat. Then he opened his eyes and shook himself.

"Are you hurt?" O'Brien said.

"I'm not hurt," muttered Derrane.

He struggled to his feet.

"It was how she slipped up in a pool of water when I turned her," he said. "She was frightened by the row ye were making and she lost her balance. I'm all right now."

He began to wipe the sand from his clothes.

"Thank God, there's no harm done," said McDonagh, examining the mare's legs. "No. She's all right. Let's go on to Madigan's."

"There's never harm done when it's needed," said Delaney.

Derrane looked at him fiercely, but he said nothing.

They walked away. The accident had sobered them a little and they went quietly. When they were near Madigan's house they halted to take counsel.

"Let you begin the talking, Dan," said Delaney to O'Brien.

"I'm satisfied," said O'Brien, "if Pat McDonagh backs me up."

"I won't let you talk alone," said McDonagh, "but it's up to Bartly himself to put in a word with the girl."

"I'll have a word with her," cried Delaney, "and a hold of her too."

"I'll see you don't," muttered Derrane.

McDonagh nudged him and whispered:

"Hold your whist, man."

There was a little pier at the western end of the strand. The shore rose steeply beyond the pier to a line of crumbling cliffs that swept round the western end of the island to the south. The small hamlet of Portoona was built in a hollow some distance west of the pier. When they reached the houses, it seemed as if they were standing beneath a sloping wall, so steeply did the earth rise in the false light to the western horizon, where the sky's rim was pale, catching the reflected shadows from the moonlit rocks.

They tied the mare to the fence in Madigan's yard. A light shone through the kitchen window. They went quietly to the door and O'Brien knocked. After a little while the door was opened.

"God save all here," O'Brien said, walking into the kitchen.

"You're welcome. You're welcome," said Mrs. Madigan from the hearth corner. "Come down here to the fire. Ye just caught us in time, for we are after saying the rosary and we were getting ready for bed. How are you, Pat, asthore? And you, Martin? Is that yourself, Bartly?"

She kept on chatting and smiling as the men sat down. Although over sixty, she was still handsome, with the tawny face that goes with pale golden hair and gleaming white teeth.

There was a great commotion, for Madigan tried to bring the visitors to the hearth, while they insisted on sitting in remote corners near the dressers and the back door. Madigan, scenting the whisky under their jerseys, was very excited. A tall, grey-haired man, he had a long, hooked nose like a Turk. Owing to some tumour on his neck, he had to hold his head backwards to one side, like a man mummified in the act of being strangled. This also affected his voice, which was pitched on a very high note, as if he were calling for help to save him from being strangled.

The commotion subsided and there was a few minutes' conversation about the weather. Then O'Brien called for a glass.

"Ah! God bless you," said Madigan, walking eagerly to the dressers, "sure it's yourself never comes empty."

"It's kind father for him to be generous," Mrs. Madigan said.

"Don't thank me, but Bartly Delaney," said O'Brien, pulling the bottle from under his jersey. "It's for him we came."

Mary Madigan, sitting on the table by the window with a picture-book open on her lap, glanced angrily towards O'Brien. Then she looked towards Delaney and flushed. She was twenty-six, Madigan's youngest child. Although she had been six years in America she had lost none of that fresh, flower-like bloom which is a characteristic of our island women; that impish laughter of the sea-blue eyes, in which nature seems to have engemmed a myriad sunbeams and the snow-white silk of the cheeks, on which she paints bright roses that are kept radiant by an innate purity of soul. Mary was tall, full-bosomed and strong-limbed, with a jutting lower lip and thick, brown hair. Her legs dangled from the table and she kept moving her right thigh back and forth restlessly. Her shoulder leaned against the wall.

As she glanced angrily at the visitors she seemed to say:

"How dare you bring this wretched suitor to my house?"

Her eyes avoided Derrane. He, on the contrary, could not take his eyes off her face. He sat in a dark corner by the back door on a small stool. His eyes were like points of fire in the gloom. Delaney also watched her furtively. He sat on a form by the dressers, leaning forward, with his elbows on his knees. His head drooped and he breathed loudly, just like a tired sheep. Now and again he raised his eyes and feasted on the sight of Mary's legs, then on the plump, round thigh that moved restlessly back and forth beneath the short blue skirt. Trembling with excitement because of this voluptuous movement, he looked upwards to her breasts, which stood out like big cups against their covering of pale blue silk. Then, overcome by the shame of lust, he would drop his eyes to the floor and breathe heavily, like an over-heated sheep, panting under her load of oily wool.

While O'Brien forced Madigan to drink glass after glass quickly, McDonagh amused himself by making pretended advances to Madigan's eldest daughter, Julia. She stood by the door of the bedroom on the right of the kitchen, giggling and twisting about as McDonagh grabbed at her. She was nearly forty and yet no more sophisticated than a child. She had rough, flaxen hair and a red face, coarsened by twenty years of hard work in the fields and on the seashore, where she gathered weeds for kelp, up to her breasts in the tide like a man. No suitor had ever cast eyes on the drudge and yet the poor simpleton longed for love. She twisted about, like a stroked cat, as the wanton McDonagh thrust at her.

"Leave her alone, you wicked devil," said Mrs. Madigan, playfully threatening Madigan with the tongs.

Madigan and O'Brien drank nearly all of one bottle between them in a few minutes. Madigan gulped the spirit with great zest and got intoxicated almost immediately. He began to reel about the floor, talking at random.

"I have two daughters here with me," he said, " and well I know which one ye came after. The queen of Portoona she's rightly called, God bless her. Ye're not the first band of men that came to this house after her, and some that didn't come sent messengers, but she has her mind made up to go back to New York. Well! Try your luck, men. Try your luck, I say. I'll not hinder ye. I have another daughter as well—Julia, as good a worker as ever rose from her bed at crack of dawn. Aye! And she can stay on her feet until the sun goes down and then give good service in her marriage bed. Make your choice, however, neighbours. I had ten children, but they're all lost to me bar three, between the grave and America. And Mary is going back unless ye can stop her. I had a good boat and I brought her to the midwife's pier in cargo ten times. Two of them in God's Paradise and eight living. Make a drop o' punch for yourself, Kate, my hearty."

He embraced his wife, who told him laughingly to behave himself. O'Brien emptied the bottle into a mug, which he gave to Mrs. Madigan. She set about making punch. McDonagh gave the third bottle to O'Brien, who passed it round the company. It was soon empty.

"I'll go and get a gallon of potheen," said Delaney.

"What for?" said Mary sharply. "I think you have enough drunk! Save your money."

"Money!" cried Delaney, jumping to his feet. "What do I care what I spend? I have lashin's of money."

"Ha! More power to you, Bartly," cried Madigan.

"Go to bed, father," said Mary. "You're drunk. You'll be sick in a minute, same as you were the night that other man came here. I don't want anybody coming here looking for me."

"What do I care for the other man?" cried Delaney furiously. "I'm different. I have thirty acres of land and plenty of stock and money saved. I'm as good a worker as ever handled a spade or cast a net over a boat's stern!"

"True for you, Bartly," said O'Brien.

"True for you," said Madigan, shaking Delaney by the hand.

"Come with me for a gallon," cried Delaney.

"You're wasting your money as far as I'm concerned," said Mary.

"Come with me, Madigan, to the sheebeen," cried Delaney, now in a drunken frenzy. "I'll show you how I can spend money. Let ye drink till morning and I'll pay."

"Let Pat McDonagh go with you," said Madigan. "It would be a shame for me to go, seeing the reason of your visit."

Delaney and McDonagh left the house. O'Brien took Madigan by the hand and began to praise Delaney:

"You wouldn't get a better husband for your daughter in the whole parish," he said. "What does it matter about the colour of his hair? I wish I had a horse the colour of his hair. Your daughter will have a good neighbour, too, for my Kate is next door to Bartly, and a better woman than my Kate never stepped in shoes. For God's sake take advice and make this match, in God's holy name."

"If I had the say, I'd make it and a thousand welcomes, for either daughter," cried Madigan, "but it's herself has the say."

O'Brien, Madigan and Mrs. Madigan began to talk, all together, holding hands and embracing one another. The punch had gone to Mrs. Madigan's head. They paid no attention to what they said. They were all in that extravagant state of joy which comes from an occasional tipple.

Mary left the table and stood beside Derrane.

"Have you nothing to say?" she said angrily.

Her bosom heaved. Derrane leaned back and stared at her intently. He did not speak, but the muscles of his face and throat were all in motion. One could see that he had been a soldier from the way he held his body, erect from the hips, with the shoulders squared and level, the head correctly poised on the neck. His dark eyes seemed aflame.

"Why did you come here?" she whispered.

"I want to talk to you," he whispered.

"What is it?"

"Something I want to say."

"Well! Then, say it."

"I can't here."

"Why?"

"People are listening."

She shrugged her shoulders and folded her arms on her bosom. Her shoulders were trembling. They were silent for a little while, staring at one another. The other voices became louder and more unbalanced. Julia crept along the wall, watching the two lovers in the corner and grinning. She suddenly burst out laughing and covered her face with her hands. Mary started and whispered to Derrane.

"Maybe I'll talk to you later outside," she said. "I'll try to manage it. Wait outside for me."

She walked smartly towards Julia, swaying at the hips. Her body looked beautiful in motion. Derrane pursued her with his eyes, greedily. Julia, seeing her sister approach, laughed aloud once more and then ran into the bedroom, clumsily stumbling against the half open door, which she tried to close behind her. Mary, however, was too quick. She forced her way into the bedroom and closed the door. There was a muffled scream and the sound of hands slapping something soft. The three who were talking loudly by the hearth took no notice. Derrane suddenly jumped to his feet and went out into the yard. There he met Delaney and McDonagh returning with a gallon of potheen in a sack.

"Who's that?" McDonagh said.

Derrane moved away without answering and McDonagh went into the kitchen with Delaney. They put the gallon jar of potheen on the floor near the fire.

"Hoigh! God spare your health," cried Madigan. "It's a night 'til morning now, sure enough."

"Devil roast the first man that falls," cried O'Brien.

They began to drink once more, passing the glass rapidly. They coughed as the pale, raw spirit burned their throats and descended to their stomachs like an enraged enemy of reason and conscience. They got to their feet, sat down and rose again without purpose. They sang, shouted, danced, fell on the floor, rolled about and made protestations of their love to one another. There was a tumult as if a band of madmen had broken loose from their confinement and had broached a wine cellar. Mrs. Madigan was almost as tipsy as the men. She ogled Pat McDonagh, who fumbled at her thighs, whenever he staggered towards her in his drunken wanderings.

Delaney was the only one who retained a small element of reason. He pursued Madigan about the floor, begging him to talk about the match.

"Bring her here, so that I can ask her," he kept repeating.

"She's set on America," Madigan would say. "Ah! God help you, poor man, she's set on America."

Tears rolled down his cheeks as he cried:

"I'd rather have you as a son-in-law than a king's eldest son."

Maudlin with liquor, he embraced Delaney as his best loved friend. He wept aloud and asked God to strike him dead if he didn't love Delaney more than any man on earth.

"Ask her yourself," he said. "Try to put the come hither on her with word of mouth."

"Bring her to me," cried Delaney. "Let me get a hold of her and I'll ask her."

"Drink, you unnatural son of a beggar-woman," cried O'Brien, "and don't mind the woman."

He sat on the floor by the gallon jar and took McDonagh by both hands. They began to sing a song.

"I want to marry your daughter, Madigan," shouted Delaney, getting furious.

The four of them got to their feet and jostled about the floor. It was hard to say whether they were going to fight or to embrace one another. Then they fell apart, exhausted by this effort. Madigan fell backwards, rolled under the table, sighed and became unconscious in a drunken stupor. O'Brien tried to stay his fall, but failed and fell himself down on the floor. He laughed hysterically and then put his head on his chest and began to sing, waving his hands. McDonagh also sang, with his head in Mrs. Madigan's lap and his hands caressing her old breasts.

Delaney, breathing heavily, like a hot sheep, staggered to the door of the bedroom. He began to knock on the door, swaying backwards and forwards.

"I want to marry a young girl," he muttered.

Julia laughed within the room. This excited him.

"Who's laughing at me?" he cried. "Laughing at me? I'll show you."

Roused by this insult, he seized the door knob and threw open the door. He plunged into the room. In the dim light, he could see the white bed on which a girl was sitting, her arms clasping her knees. It was Julia, but he was too drunk to recognize the difference between her and Mary.

"I have you now," he cried, plunging towards the bed.

Julia giggled and covered her face with her hands and turned towards the wall. He threw himself on top of her and began to fumble at her body. She struck playfully at him and twisted about, but she did not speak.

Mary had been standing by the door, listening to the people in the kitchen, waiting for an opportunity to leave the house. When Delaney entered she ran into the kitchen. She glanced round the kitchen and then went on tiptoe out into the yard. Derrane was nowhere to be seen. She stood on the stile that led to a path towards the cliffs. She looked all round, but could not see him. Had he gone? She began to tremble.

"Martin," she called. "Where are you?"

Suddenly he rose up before her from the earth, like a ghost evoked by her cry. The land sloped sharply downwards from the house, for about two hundred yards, and then it rose abruptly to the left, ending in a cliff, whose topmost point stood against the sea's horizon in the moonlight like a dog's head. To the right, the land continued to descend, gently, to the pier and Portoona strand. The earth here was crusted with flat limestone rocks, lying in narrow rows, like long flat teeth, with lank faded grasses and small briars in the slits. Down in the hollow there were no rocks, except a single massive granite boulder, surrounded by a patch of grass. Derrane had been lying in the shade of this boulder. Now he stood against the horizon of the sea like a mast, dark compared to the grey rocks that gleamed white in the moonlight.

The night was very still. The sea made a lapping sound near by against the cliff, like water at the bottom of a barrel that is trundled. In the distance it simmered on the beach. A faint breeze, lazy and irregular, swayed the pale, uncropped grasses and made the ferns and small briars rustle, like the scraping of mice in a loft, as their tendrils moved back and forth over the surface of the flat rocks. The air was perfumed and so pure that it made the lungs delight in breathing. Oh! So pure that it was hard to believe that sin or pain could exist on this earth.

He waved and she ran towards him. He took her by the hands and led her to the shelter of the boulder. They stood facing one another, their bodies touching, behind the great mass of granite that was taller than their heads. They did not speak, but they both trembled, just like the ferns that trembled at the rock's base under the wind's caress. Her head was bare, and the breeze, playing about her hair, swayed the little tresses that hung loose, so that they rippled back and forth, just like young blades of grass waving in Spring-time. A long strand drifted over her eyes. She put up her hand to remove it. Then he shuddered and put his arms around her waist. She leaned back and closed her eyes. The moonlight shone on her throat. He began to whisper his love. She groaned and drew her hands slowly down along his body to his waist. Then she laughed and pressed his body close to hers, leaning back from the waist. He gently bared her breasts. They were golden in the moonlight and the dark nipples looked like buds about to burst in Spring with the sun's heat. Then he caressed her breasts and whispered to her, stooping forward slowly, until her waist lay between his widespread thighs and his breath was on her lips. He laid her gently down on the pale, uncropped grass beneath the boulder. She held up the two gleaming bowls of her breasts towards his face and whispered:

"Love me, sweetheart. I belong to you."

Then he took her unto him and they wantoned on the grass that whispered like fondled silk beneath their leaping bodies. Their cries of love rose into the night like prayers of thanksgiving and of triumph to the divine source of life. Then he lay still with his face between her breasts. She caressed his hair and then she put her cheek against his head and sang to him.

Suddenly they heard a shriek. For a moment there was silence and then again the shriek rang out, unseemly on the pure air. They sat up, startled.

"I'll kill the ruffian," cried a voice.

"My God!" said Mary. "That's my brother. That's Michael. What's the matter?"

Derrane jumped to his feet and listened. Now many voices shouted in the house. Derrane took a step in that direction, but she caught him by the knee and held him. "Don't go yet, Martin," she whispered, rising and clutching him. "Stay with me. Let's go away together."

"We can't go now, Mary. Where could we go?"

"Oh! Anywhere. Don't leave me. Take me with you."

"But where? I have no house. I have no money."

"Come to America. I have money. Come with me."

"I'd be ashamed."

"No. No. You must come. Do you love me? Tell me."

"I love the ground you walk on."

"Then you must come. Oh! You must come, Martin."

"Yes, I'll come."

"Come to-morrow. No, it's to-day now. Come to-day with me. The steamer comes from the town to-day. It will take us. Will you come to-day?"

"Yes, I'll come," he whispered, trembling, hardly able to speak. "Oh! I love you, Mary, but I'm so ashamed, not having a penny. I was ashamed to come and ask your father for you."

"What does it matter? Only us two. Kiss me."

The shouting was now louder and they heard a man groan as they kissed. Julia ran shrieking through the yard.

"Don't tell anyone," said Mary. "Just get ready and I'll meet you on the pier when the steamer is leaving. Promise me on your soul that you'll be there."

"On my soul!"

"Say it again. Oh, Martin, I couldn't live without you another day. I love you so much. You won't go back on me. Say it again."

"On my soul. Darling! Sure, I'd swim the ocean to come to you. My sweet pulse!"

They embraced wildly and then Derrane stooped and ran towards the pier. With her head thrown back and her hands on her bosom where his head had lain, she looked after him, whispering and laughing. The moon had now grown dim, veiled by the approach of dawn. The sea had turned black, and to the west the land swept upwards in a rigid wall, all black, to the sky, where the dawn mists were gathering, like billowing, grey wreaths.

She ran to her sister, who met her at the stile.

"What happened, Julia?" she cried.

Julia began to tap her on the bosom, just like a hare struggling impotently in a hound's jaws.

"Michael came home from fishing and caught Bartly Delaney on the bed with me," she sobbed. "I think he has killed him. They're all fighting with Michael now."

"Shut your mouth," said Mary.

She dragged Julia after her.

"I don't want to go in there," cried Julia, resisting. "I'm afraid of Michael. Bartly did nothing to me. Cross my heart he didn't."

"Shut up, you idiot," cried Mary.

Julia's rough, grey dress was disarranged and torn at

the bosom. Sobbing, she allowed herself to be led into the house.

"What's going on here?" said Mary. "Be quiet, I say."

Young Michael Madigan stood against the wall near the back door, struggling to break loose from O'Brien and McDonagh who were holding him.

"Let me go," he shouted. "I'll kill him."

"Be quiet," said O'Brien. "Haven't you done enough to him? Try and pacify him, Mary! He won't listen to us."

Young Madigan's dark eyes looked startled, like a person just awakened from a horrid nightmare. His trousers were flecked with the white scales of fish. His shirt was about his neck and his naked chest was stained with blood from Delaney's face. Delaney lay prostrate on the floor. Blood oozed from a gash in his forehead. His right arm was thrown out far among the bream that had fallen from young Madigan's upturned basket. The silvery sides of the bream and their pink, wedge-shaped tails glistened in the lamplight. Their half-open, dark mouths and their circular eyes, so glassy, seemed to gape at the strange company. The odour of their briny flesh was heavy and almost sickening.

"God help me, I can do nothing to him," Mrs. Madigan wailed by the hearth. "Oh, God help me."

Madigan was sitting on the floor, gesticulating with both hands, but unable to rise.

Mary went over to her brother and said in a low voice: "Keep quiet, Michael. What are you shouting for?"

He became silent at once.

"Let him go," she said to O'Brien and McDonagh.

They loosed him. Young Madigan pulled down his shirt.

"What on earth is the matter with you, Michael?" she said.

"I found him in the room with Julia," cried Michael. "I'll kill him."

He was about to rush at Delaney once more, but she pushed him back. Delaney raised his head.

"There isn't a man on the island as good as me," he shouted. "Where is the bastard that hit me?"

He pawed the floor with his outstretched hand. The fish began to slip about. He shook his head. The blood flowed down into his eyes. He put up his hand, touched the blood and then looked at it.

"Blood!" he shouted. "I'm murdered. Who killed me? Where is the murderer?"

He tried to rise, but only succeeded in plunging headlong among the fish and the fishing lines which had rolled from the basket.

"Look after him, you two," Mary said. "Come into the room with me, Michael."

She brought her brother into the small bedroom on the left. He sat on the bed and whispered:

"I couldn't help it, Mary. He was pawing at her on the bed and she laughing like an idiot. I wanted to kill him. God forgive me, I'd have killed him only for they stopping me."

"Was it you cut him?"

"No. I think it was how he fell against the edge of the table when he was trying to make for the door."

"It doesn't matter, Michael. I'm the cause of all this row, but I'm going away to-morrow, so you can have peace."

"You're going away to-morrow, Mary?" he whispered, looking at her wistfully. "Where are you going?"

"No. It's to-day I'm going, Michael. I'm going with Martin."

"With Martin Derrane?"

"Don't tell anyone, Michael. I'll say I'm just going for a week to the town. Oh, I love him, Michael! You won't be cross with me?"

They put their arms round one another and they began to sob.

"I know he loves you too, Mary, so it's all right, only my father wouldn't hear of him coming for you. I'll come to the town on the steamer with you."

"I'll always love you, Michael," she whispered, wiping the tears from her eyes. "We'll come home when we have enough money saved to buy a farm."

"I'll always love you too, Mary."

Again they embraced and wept.

In the kitchen, O'Brien and McDonagh washed the cut on Delaney's head with potheen from the jar. He moaned when the harsh spirit entered the wound. Mrs. Madigan still wailed by the hearth, but she was unable to move. Madigan snored on the floor. Julia crouched over the fish and giggled as she stroked their slippery sides with her finger. Then they raised Delaney to his feet. Julia ran into her bedroom and closed the door. McDonagh poured the remainder of the whisky into a bottle.

"Well, good night now, and God bless you all," he said.

"Safe journey to you," Mary answered from the bedroom.

Nobody else spoke. Delaney's feet dragged along the ground as they led him from the house. As they passed the window of Julia's bedroom she put out her head and whispered:

"Good night, sweetheart."

Then she giggled and closed the window. O'Brien and McDonagh began to titter. They propped Delaney against the fence where the mare was tied. Then they doubled up with laughter. The mare whinnied and pawed the ground nervously.

"He wanted the young one, but it was the stripper he got," cried O'Brien, thumping McDonagh in the chest.

"He didn't come away empty in any case," laughed McDonagh. "Upon my soul! He's nippy enough when he gets the chance. You couldn't see his tail with dust and he sneaking into Julia's bed. The ruffian should be put in jail for raping the innocent."

"You're right," bawled O'Brien. "He should be cut, the scoundrel. Our wives are not safe with him about."

"Ho, the rascal!" said McDonagh. "If he gets his way, he'll turn the whole parish into a bawdy house."

Delaney drooped over the fence, his head and arms hanging down the far side. He sickened, as if in answer to their ribald laughter. Then they loaded him on to the mare's back. The mare shivered. She smelt at her strange load and pawed the ground. He lay on her back like a corpse, his head and arms hanging down on one flank, his legs on the other. She smelt one side and then the other. They led her away slowly.

Dawn was breaking as they passed the strand. Curlews were on the wing and their sharp, eerie cries re-echoed in the hollowed cliffs.

Delaney's face looked yellow in the light of dawn. A great blotch of blood had congealed, like red paint on his forehead. His limp carcass looked ever so unseemly against the mare's silken, black hide.

They put the mare in her field and then they sat under the fence to have a drink. Delaney tossed about the field, trying to walk and falling in a heap each time he tried to take a step. The other two paid no heed to him. They drank from their bottle and clasped hands and sang a song of love.

Delaney floundered about the field, muttering:

"I want to marry a young girl. I have thirty acres and plenty of stock and . . ."

It was like a grotesque dance, the drunken leaping of that withered man.

### XVII

HERE ends my tale, if such it can be called. It ends in failure, for I did not find what I set out to find: the meaning of the word truth. Unless it is success to feel convinced that Pilate was a gentleman, when he washed his hands and thought of his appointment at his club on being irritated by the ravings of Jewish rabbis, whose shekels had been threatened by a revolutionary. I mean that I have failed as far as others are concerned, but as far as I myself am concerned I have succeeded in a marvellously proper way.

I have told the truth about myself, and in this way I have warded off my enemies, who are those that by their flattery would shackle me with the traits of their mediocrity. I have torn the veil of sanctity from my face for those who do not know me and I have deprived my friends of the pleasure of adverse criticism. It is pleasant for others to think of a man that the world finds him good, for then they are amused by pricking his conceit. And best of all, should I be considered worth a biography, I have robbed grave-robbers of their beastly loot.

Whether I die drunk or sober, honoured with fame and fortune, or disdained as a villainous pauper, I feel fortified by this outpouring of what had been festering in me. I have cast out my sins to make room for more serious misdemeanours. In future I'll sin with greater cunning. I have no god, but I have shamed the devil into obedience by an exhibition of inverted pride greater than Lucifer's. I have charted my love, having put love beyond me AS THE LUXURY OF LESSER MEN. I sail forth alone on a sea that has no port of call, no land fall, nor triumphant home-coming. I sail alone, with the mutinous crew of my passions, but if I remain enough of a devil they'll add to me. And when I don't, then my throat is to their knives and I shall not squeal.

I am a fool, but I am one of the great fools, for my folly is a great concupiscence. I desire first of all the flesh and then the spirit. I reach the spirit through the flesh and not the flesh through the spirit. Let me be covered with contumely, so long as I can feel the stirring of my flesh and the stirring of flesh in response to my flesh. I have come back to the flesh from my journey into hell with a fiercer lust. My hands are on the summit of the wall and my eyes are blinded by the light beyond. Heave up, brave thighs, the rags that cover you shall be embroidered by the hand of God.

I have said good-bye to my despair, since it cannot stay the swooping of the carrion crows.

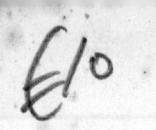